Waterline

OTHER BOOKS BY JOE SOUCHERAY

SOOCH!
Once There Was a Ballpark

Waterline

Of Fathers, Sons, and Boats

JOE SOUCHERAY

HARPER & ROW, PUBLISHERS, New York
Grand Rapids, Philadelphia, St. Louis, San Francisco
London, Singapore, Sydney, Tokyo, Toronto

To Bud

FIRST EDITION

Designed by Alma Orenstein

Library of Congress Cataloging-in-Publication Data

Soucheray, Joe.
   Waterline: of fathers, sons, and boats/Joe Soucheray.—1st ed.
      p.   cm.
   ISBN 0-06-016194-9
   1. Soucheray, Joe.   2. Journalists—United States—Biography.
3. Fathers and sons.   I. Title.
PN4874.S576A3   1989
070.92—dc19
[B]   89-45067

89 90 91 92 93 MV/HC 10 9 8 7 6 5 4 3 2 1

Acknowledgments ∿∿∿∿∿

I wish to thank the following individuals and institutions for their help and encouragement: Deborah Howell and the *St. Paul Pioneer Press Dispatch*, Jonathon Lazear, Daniel Bial, Jennifer Elias Soucheray, Jon Menth, Ray Stawikoski, Harry Zemke, Tom Juul, Tim Rumsey, and Suzanne Kampe.

1

THE SOUTH-FACING DOUBLE GARAGE DOOR was open to the alley and to the morning rain, late October rain, drops like silver bullets. The rain fell straight. It splattered hard on the blanket of fallen oak and maple leaves on the slanted concrete apron and then ran in fast streams down the alley, black and glistening streams on either side of the lumpy asphalt crown. Oversplash dampened the floor of the garage under the bow of the boat, and a few wind-tossed drops of rain made dark stains like tears on the mahogany side planking.

Nice boat: It looked like a skeleton of bleached bones, a rickety framework sitting on a trailer, the trailer the color of rust. The bow of the boat was cleaved open, the stem absent. The unfastened side planks were springy.

"If you're cold, you could wait in the house until he gets here," I told my father, J. Henry, who goes by the name of Bud. He was known as Bud as a boy, when he was thick-chested and had a head of curly black hair and a look of cocky defiance on his face (which has always been a mystery to me; he has never struck me as cocky). My breath made steam and so did Bud's. The glistening yellow leaves, the rain, the smoky puffs of our breaths, all conspired to put winter on the wind. The coming night would be good for a wood fire.

"I'm fine," Bud said, automatically, stoical that way. Offhand, I couldn't remember his ever issuing a negative report. He was sitting on his portable tripod, a British product of spindly aluminum legs and a leather seat, the kind of stool designed to use around the green in a golfing gallery. Both his hands were on the brass duck's head crown of his walking stick, the walking stick nicked up plenty, its varnish worn off in spots that showed bare wood. His hands were swollen from arthritis, and I knew that they would be cold to the touch, too, because when it came to good circulation, Bud was losing ground. Still, he looked comfortable in a bulky down jacket, navy blue, and thick, olive-colored flannel trousers, his Malones. He looked not unlike a villager that he and my mother had once taken a photograph of in Ireland, an old sodder who posed in front of the green-shuttered window of a cream-colored stone house and smiled back at the camera with a face of soft leather.

"If I didn't open the door," I said, "Ray would likely as not stay out in the alley until I did. He's not one to make himself at home. This guy is very shy, very humble."

Bud silently regarded the prospect of meeting Ray. "You need a heater in your shop," Bud said, meaning the garage.

It was lightly understood between us that I was thought to be incapable of carpentry, of shop work, so that Bud and my brothers and sisters—my two children and my wife, Jennifer, for that matter—liked to make me an example of folly whenever they could, calling the garage a shop. The same might be said of most newspapermen; it's in our genes only to write about the people who fix and build. I was thought to be competent with a hammer and little else, having never, in thirty-six years, demonstrated any inclination to skillful labor. I hadn't ever made a significant repair around the house, short of puttying windows, and yet I wanted my family to believe that I could restore a boat.

Three months earlier, in July 1984, I had hauled home, on the wild speculation that I could resurrect it, a 1938 seventeen-foot Chris Craft Deluxe utility motorboat. It was in such disintegrating condition that when I took off the cutwater—the decorative shield of stainless steel that runs vertically down the bow of the boat—the stem behind it fell to the garage floor and broke into three brittle pieces of dry-rotted oak. I was alone. I wasted one of the great double takes of my life: a slow, theatrical pan around the empty garage, my eyes returning to the pile of broken stem at my feet, lingering there and then looking up again, blinking disbelief.

Now I was learning at a rushed, forced pace. It impressed Bud to see the boat so entirely in a state of disassembly that it was little more at the moment than the framework, without a stem. That is, I presumed him to be impressed. With him, it was hard to tell. He was as guarded and reserved as I was anxious and all-confessing. We didn't look like each other, either. Bud was slope-shouldered and meaty, with thick, graying curly hair. I was tall and bony with thinning blond hair. We were waiting in the garage for Ray to bring over a new stem. The night before, I had called my father and suggested that the installation of a new stem was something he might not want to miss.

"I'd like to see that," he had said, but neutrally. And then: "I'd like to see how your shop operates."

It was in most respects a conventional garage, except for the antique motorboat taking up half of it. Garden tools, sprinklers, a half-dozen snap-on hose connections, clay pots, the lawnmower gasoline can, and a spray bottle of weed killer were orphaned on the second shelf at the end of the workbench nearest the service door. There were baby swings and carpet remnants and water toys and cross-country skis in the rafters.

My double-shelved workbench ran almost the length of the west wall of the garage, black tar paper between the studs. The countertop, the bench itself, had been given over exclusively to boat work. I had paints lined up there, as well as solvents, glues, caulks, tools, China bristle brushes, coffee cans full of brass screws, sandpaper, sanding blocks, the radio, and a plastic, compartmentalized, thirty-drawer assortment of new screws, bolts, washers, grommets, and cotter pins, all brass. Power tools were on the lower shelf, two drills, a hot-air paint-removing gun and three sanders, two conventional orbital sanders, and my favorite, a Makita block finishing sander—"fits in the palm of your hand." I had read about the Makitas in a boat-building magazine and bought mine on sale after I saw *Makita* spelled out in a thin tube of red neon glass in the window of Seven Corners Hardware in downtown St. Paul.

The paint-splattered radio was on low—Tina Turner singing "What's Love Got to Do with It?" A good, rhetorical question, I thought, especially for my curious task.

It was my shop, all right, the center of my action for two years, a place with my markings. For luck, I nailed a Montreal Canadiens matchbook cover into the lintel above the service door. The *C* on the sweater of a Canadien resembles a horseshoe. Nailed to one of the wall studs above the workbench was an exploded drawing of a Chris Craft cabin cruiser, a 1955 El Capitan, although it was intended to apply generically to all Chris Craft hulls. The drawing was entitled "Nomenclature of Hull Parts, Chris Craft Corporation, Algonac, Mich., Drawing No. B-12135."

Nailed to the next stud over was a magazine page from the April/May 1982 *Small Boat Journal* that showed a Chris Craft factory photograph of two 1939 seventeen-foot Chris Craft utilities, a Deluxe and a Standard. Although a year older, my boat was virtually identical to the Deluxe utility in the photograph. I had only to point out the photograph to the curious souls who wandered in and out of the garage, my shop, to show what it was I was attempting to resurrect.

Bud didn't need a picture. He knew the boat. He owned one exactly like it from approximately 1957 through 1962, a period of life that I have come to think of in terms of a snapshot, a photo album period of life, everybody in their prime then. Bud could imagine more easily than most what my boat was supposed to look like, how it behaved in the water, how it looked underway, how it smelled and felt, and what it sounded like with water spurting out the little copper nub of its exhaust pipe.

I ran a trouble light from the workbench to the front of the boat and hung it on a seam batten, full of myself, I suppose, for knowing the difference between a seam batten and, say, a sheer batten. Thanks to Drawing No. B-12135, I also knew the difference between a monkey rail and a grub beam. I watched my father out of the corner of my eye. He rarely complained about the pain in his arthritic knees. Sometimes, though, when he thought nobody was looking, he hung his head, especially in such foul, damp weather, just hung his head and stared at the floor, biting his lower lip. He was sixty-seven.

My own daughter, Emily, just six, fought off a bout of rheumatoid arthritis over the summer, something called

Still's disease. Looking at Bud now, reminded of his creaking joints, I wondered if she would wrestle with the disease all her life the way he had.

"At what point," I asked Bud, "do you suppose people give up on these boats?"

"I would have thought by now," Bud said, looking at the peeled-open bow. "I've never heard of anyone having to put in a new stem. Judas Priest, a new stem."

"Or rear braces," I said. Massive rot had also eaten away the rear braces behind the transom boards.

"Where would you be without Ray?" he said.

"In serious trouble," I said. I was making a shelf on the front deck beams, laying a piece of board over the exposed beams. After the fashion of a surgeon, I spread a rag out on the board and laid out the tools I thought we'd need: screwdrivers, open-ended wrenches, and three new brass carriage bolts to attach the forefoot of the stem to the keel.

"And there's no rot in the keel?" Bud said, looking up from a crack he had been studying in the concrete floor.

I was going to tell him about chemically repairing a small section of soft wood, but then we heard Ray. I had gotten so I could tell the sound of his approach. I swear, his tires splashed in the alley in a certain tentative way. He pulled up slowly and parked on the apron. Ray opened the tailgate of his maroon Plymouth station wagon and put the new stem under his jacket. When he got inside the garage he uncovered the new stem and held it out for me to see.

"Ray Stawikoski, Bud Soucheray," I said. But my eyes were on the stem, the elegant stem.

Ray was sixty-four, a retired pattern maker. He was built along the same lines as my father—stocky, with broad, sloping shoulders. His beige poplin jacket was marked with slanted splotches of rain. He wore a blue corduroy baseball-style cap. Beneath the brim of the cap he looked as round-faced and pontifical as John Paul II.

"He's doing quite a job," Ray said.

"Quite a project, I'll say," my father said.

They were similar in height and weight, thick-wristed old coots with salt-and-pepper hair, although Ray was going more quickly bald. They suddenly both seemed shy, too, and unsure of what to say.

I held the new stem. It was white oak and smelled of old lumberyards. I knew only vaguely how Ray had made it, first roughing it out on a band saw, then hand-planing it, and finally hand-carving the rabbits—the indented edges down either side of the stem into which fit each of the six side planks on both sides of the hull. It was to become the most vital piece in the boat, without which there could be no boat, not to mention the idiom that kept coming in to my mind, "from stem to stern."

"You did good, saving the old pieces," Ray said. His speech patterns were as simple and as repetitive as an old baseball manager's. Casey Stengel without the malapropisms. "I always tell people, 'Save the old pieces, save the old pieces, give me something to work with.' You did good, saving the old pieces, Joe. I don't know, Joe, I hope it works. It looks good. We'll see. I did the best I could."

Ray always brought along his own tools, in wooden boxes and compartments, like a printer's California job case. He preferred to stay out of the installation process, but he was so intrigued by the stem that he agreed to waive his hands-off policy. I had the topmost side planking removed, leaving only the battens. The remaining planks were unfastened from the bow back to a point behind the front seat. I used two-by-fours to hold the sprung planking away from the gaping hole where the old stem had been. I was careful not to bend the planking too far out of the way. I didn't bother prying out the battens. They were thin pieces of oak, and we could hold them out of the way.

"Like a puzzle," I said.

Bud got out of the way, careful not to block Ray's light. I positioned the new stem in place, and Ray penciled marks on the forefoot where he intended to drill through the new oak. Ideally, we wanted to come through the new stem with bolt holes that would line up with the holes in the knee, that extension of the keel that upturns like the shoe of an elf. The stem came so sharply to a V shape that drilling holes through the point of the V was like drilling holes on the point of a pin.

"Can you do it, Ray?"

"I can do that," Ray said.

I climbed inside, pulling the trouble light in behind me. I felt caged and cramped. The plan was simple. I would do the running and climbing and fetching and maneuvering in the tight spaces. Ray would perform more delicate chores—the impossible drilling. I slathered epoxy on the outside of the knee. Ray fit the stem up against the knee and drilled through his premarked holes. The epoxy mixed with the sawdust from Ray's freshly drilled holes. Bud then held the stem so that Ray could tap the first shoulder bolt through with a hammer.

"Shit!" I said.

"What's that, Joe?" Ray said, but calmly, always calm.

"We're too close to the edge of the knee with the first hole," I said. I couldn't know that until the first bolt appeared because of the mess of epoxy and sawdust.

"That's the H of it," Ray said. "I've never done this before. That's just the H of it."

"It's not that bad," I said. "I can still get a nut on there."

"Let's drive the other two through and see what she looks like," Ray said.

He did, a second and then the third. I placed a washer and nut on each one and tightened each one down, but not firmly. The stem still had to be wiggled and jimmied so that it perfectly reflected the front angle of the original, allowing each side plank to fit smoothly into the rabbit on each side of the stem. We were fated to be off some, but not by much. I climbed out of the boat and lined up each seam batten, applying a dab of epoxy to each batten before screwing the batten to the stem. At the factory in Algonac, Michigan, the battens were nailed to the stem. And then, one by one, starting with the bottom boards (which were the most difficult because they were so unyielding), we drew the boards into the stem and fastened them.

I don't know if that's the way they did it in Algonac. I don't know if that's the way the professional restorers do it. I only know what we did. And that it worked. And that I was filled with the sense that, within reason, anything old and sentimentally valuable can be fixed. The boat suddenly seemed to be taking on its own sweet charmed life, and I could not help but notice the satisfied smile on my old man's face. For truth be told, boats were the bottom line for us, me and him and boats down through the years.

When we were through, Ray jostled the stem and the entire boat shook at the touch of his hand. "I think you got something here now," Ray said.

All that went before it and after it took hours, days, months, and years—a lifetime. The stem surgery itself took only an hour or so.

Before he left, Ray gave me the old stem, three pieces of rot, glued together with Elmer's.

2

I BOUGHT MY BOAT from a banker named Jon Menth, who bought it purely on the assumption that I would, in fact, buy it from him. Old-boat hobbyists are in the business of constant speculation, sometimes telepathically. Menth owned a similar utility and knew that I desperately wanted one. He bought the one that became mine from the proprietor of a farmhouse on the Minnesota River bottoms, near Chaska, Minnesota, south and a little west of Minneapolis.

Menth, one of the charter members of my regional Land O' Lakes chapter of the Antique and Classic Boat Society of North America, reported that he was the first of three customers who simultaneously, it appeared to him, raced up the rutted dirt lane to the farm place after each of the competitors had telephoned on a classified ad in the *Minneapolis Star and Tribune*. As much as I faithfully scoured the same ads, this one I had overlooked.

Menth doesn't merely read the classified ads. He analyzes them. And then he applies a mysterious and virtually scientific intuition on classifieds where he detects error. For example: My boat was advertised as a 1938 six-teen-foot Chris Craft utility. Menth moistened his finger, or chanted, or burned a length of red yarn, or did whatever it is he does when he smells something amiss. And then he dialed.

"Are you sure about that length?" Menth asked whoever was now in his clutches. Menth, forty-one, as gentle-voiced as storyteller Garrison Keillor, was the kind of banker you could interrupt by phone while he was closing a home or negotiating a commercial loan and he would whisper into the mouthpiece, "I've got a little Gar Wood tucked away." Antique and classic boats consumed him. Jennifer, having gotten glimpses of his almost surreal calmness, his evenhandedness, his curious leftover-1960s page-boy haircut, harbored such strong suspicions that Menth must have been a prisoner of war—where else, she wondered, might he have developed such a meditative glow?—that once I even asked him if he had served in Vietnam. He had not.

There was another, less public Menth. Just below the surface of his professional gentleness and soothing manner was the hard, cold soul of a bounty hunter. Menth was considered to be among the best, the hungriest, and the most relentless boat scavengers in the upper Midwest; I had heard him tell stories of renting small planes and having the pilot fly low over lakes in northern Wisconsin, of scuba diving under boat houses, of adventuring across frozen lakes on snowmobiles to peek into frosted boat house windows.

It was unlikely that Chris Craft produced a sixteen-foot utility in 1938, although, unlike automobile manufacturers, boat builders (even the ones in mass production) were convinced easily enough to build whatever a heart desired. Also peculiar to the boat-building industry in the 1930s and 1940s was the casual year-to-year model change, so that it took precise readings of a boat's serial number, as well as historical documentation from the manufacturer, to determine the year in which a boat was made. Many people who sell boats that they inherited with a piece of property or were bequeathed by a grandfather have no idea what it is they are selling or when it was built.

Still, seventeen feet was the standard length of Chris Craft utilities in the late 1930s. Menth took a wad of folding money and raced out to the farmhouse in his black El Camino, a modern-day Paladin answering a telegram. Upon his arrival he discovered just what he had anticipated, a 1938 seventeen-foot Chris Craft utility. Menth went directly to an engine stringer—one of two longitudinal supports in the bilge onto which the engine is bolted—for a serial number while his less-enterprising competitors stood around and studied the condition of the boat, which was appalling.

Best of all, Menth could tell from a practiced look beyond the surface wear and tear that it was a Deluxe model, as opposed to the more spartan Standard edition. Without dickering, Menth handed the asking price of $600 to the owner, dropped the trailer onto the hitch of his El Camino and was back down the lane before the other prospective buyers could know what they had missed. Menth trailered it to the home of his parents, on Smithtown Bay, on Lake Minnetonka.

In the parlance of the boat-collecting game, the utility was thus "tucked away."

It was to the Smithtown Bay address that my son, Andy, and I reported on July 15, 1984. We went out right after supper. It was the red-letter day that Emily got out of the hospital. I felt stirrings of guilt for leaving virtually as soon as Emily returned home. I could not then explain the compulsion I felt to bring that boat, which I had yet to see, to my own house.

The Menth driveway was half in shade, sunlight filtering through the long stringy branches of willow trees around the drive. Moisture gathered in streamers in the warm, humid air, leaving wispy trades of haze over the marshy grasses on the other side of Smithtown Bay Road, where there was a small lake, Lake Virginia. Menth, looking like a country gentleman, was leaning both arms on the covering boards of the boat and gazing into it—maybe to hide an understandable smirk—as we drove up.

"Here she is," he said, launching into the peculiar boat language that is as foreign to an outsider as the strange clicking and clucking language of the Kalahari bushmen. I once bought a brass Sherwood water pump for a Chris Craft engine from a man named Bob Swanson who, when he began speaking, so startled me that I looked around us expecting to find another person. Swanson had the habit of referring to mechanical parts as "him," as when he handed me the pump and said, "Be careful now, he's full of grease." In explaining what he had done to determine that the pump worked, Swanson indicated the four bolts that secured the end plate of the pump and said, "I took these four guys off and looked inside him. His gears look good." Walking me through his fields north of St. Paul, where he lived in an old farmhouse on grounds scattered with the remains of at least a dozen derelict hulls, Swanson pointed to a Lyman outboard runabout sitting on the ground. "He's a good one," he said.

And now I was hearing it again, from Menth.

"It's a good piece," Menth said, "a lucky find."

I could smell Lake Minnetonka as we got out of the car, see it in slivers of glaring reflection through the trees, sense it in the distant sounds of boats and water lapping the shore. Despite its neglect, the boat seemed entirely in its proper element, a thing wet and waiting to be under way. Just the first look indicated that it was indescribably in ruin, although in the first moment of discovery and excitement I didn't absorb the full implications of deterioration.

In the blush of seeing the boat for the first time I saw only what I wanted to see, a Chris Craft utility boat. There was only one glaring problem that I noticed immediately. It had a wrap-around Plexiglas windshield, presumably in deference to one of its owners having grown weary of getting splashed in even modest waves and wind. The original flat, folding, square-cornered windshield that gives such boats their antique charm had probably been thrown away. The correct, original windshield on any style or make of antique or classic boat is just about as important as the correct engine or instruments or the actual wood itself; the windshield is by far the most valued piece of hardware on such craft, and it is the bane of the hobby to find it missing. It would be as though antique automobile enthusiasts routinely discovered Model A Fords that had had the original dash replaced with digital instrumentation from a fiberglass-kit car.

"Menth," I said, hardly needing to remind him, "there's no windshield."

The idea that windshields routinely worth $1,000 in the 1980s were thrown out purely to achieve a drier ride is so inconceivable to hobbyists and collectors that they often tell crazy stories about the custom. I know better, though. The stories aren't necessarily crazy. I saw it happen once myself, a man parting with his windshield. It happened while I was growing up. We shared our dock with our neighbor, Bill Liedl, who kept a 1949 eighteen-foot Chris Craft Sportsman hanging on hooks next to our utility. One Saturday morning we watched him lug a box down to the dock. The box had SEARS printed on it in big block letters. Liedl took a new plastic windshield out of the box and set it on the dock. Then he removed the Chris Craft windshield, a V-shaped glass windshield with chrome fittings.

The new windshield so drastically changed the shape and flowing lines of Liedl's boat that it suddenly looked incapable of gathering speed. The boat looked fat, complacent. Liedl next gathered up the cardboard box and the original windshield, walked off the dock and across our yard, and heaved the armload of goods into what we called the swamp. It hadn't been swamp for years but was more accurately a weedy no-man's-land between our place and the public easement. Sneaky Bill probably knew we were watching and shot a quick, nervous glance at our windows as he walked across the yard.

This is all a long way of saying that evidently a boat must offer other virtues if the prospective buyer is willing to overlook the absence of the real windshield. Sitting on a trailer in Menth's driveway, the utility about to become mine had that same fat, out-of-character look as the old Liedl boat, but in all other respects I saw what I wanted to see, an original bow light, lifting rings, quarter brasses, rub rails, cutwater, gas cap, and exhaust trim ring—"jewelry," in the parlance of the boat game. The dash was a hodgepodge of ridiculous equipment added over the years, a jagged hole cut into the mahogany for, of all things, a Philco automobile radio. The radio's dial was punched out, shards of faded yellow plastic around the edges, as though struck by a cartoon fist. There was a bilge pump switch on the dash; bilge pump switches might be more discreetly located. The thick black steering wheel was baked by the sun, cracked and bleached. Menth watched me look the boat over.

"It's all there," he said, meaning to say that it was all there after the application of countless hours of restoration, of blood, sweat, tears, money.

"But it's rough," I said, lamely trying to sustain bargaining leverage.

"I think it's solid," Menth said.

"I don't know," I said, fighting my own doubts, "there's no windshield." I wondered what I was getting into.

"I think I know where there is a windshield or two tucked away," he said. I wasn't surprised.

My eyes wandered over the boat and back to the dash. The original oval instrument panel was intact, as well as the Model-T-style ignition. I tried to pull out the key from the middle of the ignition assembly, but the key was frozen in the tumbler, probably broken apart inside the tumbler. My mind raced ahead to find solutions to all the problems that kept popping up. A shooting gallery of problems. Memories flooded over me as I tried to remember Bud's old utility.

Andy walked around the boat, his arms folded, a cautious body language inherited from his mother. Menth made small talk with Andy about Little League baseball.

"What do you think, Andy?" I said.

"Great," he said.

Good boy. I had an ally. I would need Andy when Jennifer got her first look at the boat.

"I wonder how long it sat outside," I said.

Menth didn't know. It might have sat facing east, exposing the starboard side to longer, southern light. The starboard side was faded a uniform gray, and the mahogany had the texture of fuzz. The port side showed evidence of stain and yellowed, flaking varnish on the side planking under the modest flair just under the covering board, about where a passenger would have placed his left arm in repose.

The trailer, rusty, sagging, with bald tires, was last licensed in Wisconsin in 1967.

"I thought at first it might have been Bud's," Menth said. "I looked for the clues."

"It's not his," I said, "no white steering wheel, no spotlight switch next to the steering column. But it's the one most like it I've seen, not counting yours."

"I think Bud's is still out there," Menth said.

Not a chance, I thought. Too many years gone by. I climbed in, the boat rocking on the trailer. My first step in, toes first, went through the sub-floor like thin ice breaking underfoot. The mahogany box over the engine, the dog house, was warped. The seat framing was loose and the upholstery, though unbelievably enough the original blue russeloid material, was faded to the color of a high sky and so rotted that it disintegrated to the touch. The bilge was full of acorns, twigs, leaves, mice scat. A compost. True to form, the bilge smelled like a bilge, down below the dampest leaves, the smell of gasoline and oil rising like a sweet perfume when the mess was stirred to turn over the dampness of the compost.

"Well, I'll buy it," I said, laughing, knowing full well that I was going to buy it before I even showed up there.

I kept prowling around in the boat, not paying attention to Menth as he hooked the trailer to Jennifer's car. Inevitably, old boats contain as part of their abandoned cargo discarded tires, probably because old boats become trash bins. I couldn't get Menth to take the tires. Nobody wants tires. There were two pieces of wicker furniture, too, a busted canoe paddle, some nylon rope. All in all a gorgeous boat. I wrote Menth a check for $750 and presented it to him along with an agreement that I could return the boat to him in the event that I could not restore it. He agreed and we made a brief ritual of the exchange—my check for the boat now hooked to the car.

3

WE NEEDED TO TAKE ADVANTAGE of the declining light. The trailer, as beat up as the boat, had taillights, but the wiring harness had deteriorated to a few lengths of frayed wire taped carelessly to the channel iron. By the looks of the axle sag, the trailer was rolling along on the inside edges of tires that were so bald I could see the woven threads under the smooth surface of the rubber. They weren't much better than the tires tossed into the boat as trash. Actually, it was a trailer built upon a trailer, what looked to be the large square frame of an extraordinary bed set down on a smaller A-frame to which the evidently exhausted axle was attached with strap bolts. The contraption did not have brakes. It was not currently licensed, in Minnesota or Wisconsin or any other state in the union.

I was not much accustomed to trailering and thought it an adult skill acquired through age and the accumulation of great wisdom, like carving a Sunday roast or tying a proper Windsor knot. Luckily, it was a two-wheeler. Four-wheel trailers, particularly when you are backing one up, have minds of their own. I am reasonably certain that if we had set out for home with a four-wheel trailer, the television news team would have gotten onto our absence after a day or so and commissioned a helicopter to take aerial shots of us, confused and disoriented, turning circles in a shopping center parking lot out Minnetonka way, trying to get ourselves straightened out.

As we crept along, I put Andy, riding shotgun, to work as a scout, reporting every bump and sway of the old dreamboat behind us as we moved along the shore road and through the mists settling over the road as it ran in the cool shade of the willows between Lake Virginia and Lake Minnetonka. In the rearview mirror I could see only the threatening V-shaped bow bouncing in the full width of the rear window—exaggerated proof of objects in the rearview mirror appearing closer than they actually are. The trailer was tongue-heavy and put a strain on the back of the car. The task of hauling a boat made me nervous, as if I were all revved up but going slow. I tugged at my shirt where it touched lightly at my chest, and my eyes darted from the road to the rearview mirror and back to the road again.

It occurred to me that a father should subject a boy to a trailering experience, even if only once. It demonstrates industriousness. It provides a boy with the opportunity to see his father in command of what might possibly be construed as a harrowing adventure. In the spring of 1963 my father trailered home from the same lake, Minnetonka, a third- or fourth-hand twenty-two-foot Chris Craft Sportsman on a four-wheel trailer that my father commissioned to be built for him from the frame of an International panel delivery truck. That trailer alone weighed at least 1,000 pounds, a necessity for towing a boat that weighed at least 3,000 pounds. I think back with alarm that we towed such a package with nothing more muscular than a 1963 Ford Country Squire station wagon, robin's-egg blue. At the top of a rise in the village of Wayzata, the trailer disengaged from the car, and the boat and trailer rolled back down Superior Boulevard without us.

"Judas Priest!" my father said, keeping an eye on the loose rolling stock while he tried to turn around in the middle of traffic. "How in the hell did that happen?"

He went furiously hand-over-hand on the wheel, craning his neck after the disappearing boat. I remember the horns honking, the way the sun glinted off the chrome bumpers of the cars in the fateful intersection as we turned around, and the wild image of a big dark boat bouncing down the street going backwards. My father's friend Sig turned a pale shade of red and lit a cigarette.

"What do we do now, Bud?" Sig said. Sig's face was shiny with fright, except for the redness at the tip of his sharp nose.

"Judas Priest!" my father said.

"Bud," said Sig, who was an advertising executive recently transplanted from Chicago, "I'll pay whatever it costs to have this boat professionally delivered to your home. Anything. Just say the word, Bud, say it."

"Judas Priest!" my father said, straining at the wheel of the car. The intersection had become a maelstrom of noise and confusion.

"Sweet Jesus," Sig said, bracing himself with one hand on the dashboard, while he, too, craned his neck after the disappearing boat, the ash of his cigarette about to fall on the floor at my feet. "Sweet Mother of God, you need a truck to haul this boat, Henry, a big goddamn truck!"

If this went on much longer I figured I'd hear the name of everybody who sat around the table for the Last Supper. The boat and trailer came to a sudden stop against a brick retaining wall in a filling station. Its path crossed the hose that rang the bell inside the place. The bell produced the attendant, for in those days filling station attendants not only responded to the bell but appeared for action as though recently scrubbed, wearing olive-green uniforms with bow ties and motorman's caps with black, shiny visors. The eyes of this particular agent widened until they disappeared under his visor and over the top of his hairline. The bell had summoned him just in time to see a boat shooting backwards on the concrete behind the gas pumps.

We came recklessly into the lot, and my father hit the brakes so hard that the car lurched, throwing us forward. Then he remembered himself and got out of the car as though nothing unusual had happened, although he gave himself away with huge dark stains of perspiration under each arm. He gave the still-frozen station attendant a hardy wave that evidently constituted an explanation. We hooked the boat up and took off again, cautiously though, with the good sense to be intimidated by the huge, menacing presence behind us.

"What's so funny?" Andy asked me.

"Nothing," I said, still lost in that afternoon. Andy nodded, intending to let my amusement remain private. I quickly chimed in with the story of the boat breaking away from the car, embellishing it with slapstick and astonishment until we were both laughing.

"Are you happy with this boat?" Andy asked. He had his seatbelt on but he was turned comfortably sideways in his seat, facing me, the sun making a backlit halo of coppery light through his blond curly hair.

"I am at that," I said.

I was happy that at age ten he had even thought to ask such a question. He had heard plenty about the old boats and seemed willing to be captivated by them, up to a point. I think he understood that if it was a boat we wanted we might have gone out and bought something modern and reliable and probably made of fiberglass or aluminum.

"At seven hundred and fifty dollars," I said, "how can you go wrong? This is the one, boy."

"A seventeen-footer," he said, "boy, a seventeen-footer will fit in our garage."

"Menth says that Bud's boat is still out there," I said. "I don't know. This one will have to be close enough because it's hard for me to believe that Bud's boat could still exist."

"I know, I know already," Andy said, heading me off from telling him for the hundredth time that my father, his grandfather, had given his 1938 seventeen-foot Chris Craft utility away in the autumn of 1962 to settle a ninety-dollar gasoline and storage bill with Johnson Boat Works, a whitewashed building with big sea-green doors a mile or so straight across the lake from our house. Andy also didn't want me to launch into any of the other countless stories that had central to them boats, motor and sail, but primarily motor. That old utility of Bud's had gotten stuck in my craw until I just had to do something about it.

What I did about it was behind us now, straining at Jennifer's car, a history lesson seventeen feet long with about a six-foot beam.

It was a priceless Minnesota summer night, as cherished as a pearl on a string. The sun stayed lazily up there in the rose-colored sky, reluctant to drop below the horizon behind us. The yellow bulbs on the fast-food places and filling stations on both sides of the highway had a carnival look to them in the warm lush air. We drove around the southern rim of the metropolitan area, past the car dealerships and the freeway hotels and shopping malls, past the bulldozed acres of land where the old ballpark, Metropolitan Stadium, had been, past the airport, over the Fort Snelling Bridge and up into Highland Park, nearly an hour's journey from Minnetonka. People were out walking. Convertible tops were down. We made a curious sight, our cargo worth a second look to most people.

We pulled up into the alley at the back of the house, leaning on the horn. The boat looked more ruined in a city alley, without the promise of water just through the trees. People came from all directions, Jennifer and Emily from our house, Jennifer's friend Keven from her house next door.

"Here it is, Emily," I said. "I'm naming it after you." Emily hid her face against her mother's jeans, being bashful. She was pale and quiet.

"What did he do now?" Keven said, looking at Jennifer. Jennifer looked like she was going into shock.

"This is terrible," Jennifer said, beginning to laugh. "This is . . . this is awful. You went running all that way tonight to bring this home?"

"Why did he do this to you?" Keven said.

Jennifer and Keven looked at each other and rolled their eyes. Jennifer hadn't wanted me to go. She had argued that my allegiance might more properly be at home on the day that Emily got out of the hospital, but more specifically she was opposed to the boat. Not that particular boat, just opposed to the notion of there being a boat around to work on. I had had other boats that had threatened to come between us. But those boats, I pointed out, were always quartered elsewhere. My argument was that every man needed a hobby.

"An obsession is more like it," she said.

"No," I said, "a hobby. Women don't need these things. Men do. I'll bet I'm the envy of every man on this block when they see this boat."

"They won't even know it's a boat," Jennifer said. "It looks like a dumpster set down on a trailer."

The key to my defense, I figured, was keeping the boat at home. And now I was home, facing music both loud and silent. I can read Jennifer's thoughts by watching her face, so I sneaked quick glances at it, a strong face, with beautifully high cheekbones and fashion-model hazel eyes. She winced at the sight of the boat, so wretched it looked in the shadows of the alley, so weathered and sagging, and, well, sad. It wasn't Jennifer's style.

"I like new things," Jennifer said. "Why can't it be new?"

She was still making a comedy of it, whining plaintively to Keven, whom Jennifer called Sister, because they were as close as sisters and because she did not have a sister of her own. Keven's husband, Chet, wandered out slowly, chewing on a toothpick. Excitement wasn't his style.

I didn't know what to do first. Although I am forever inclined to bring old things home and save them—nineteenth-century beer bottles, box cameras, British sportscars—as though I can somehow save the past, the task discombobulates me when the relic is the size of a boat. I started tossing junk out so that it landed near the trash can. Out went the tires and the wicker things and the busted canoe paddle. Out went the grease- and oil-stained bilge pump. Andy ran into the house and brought me back a dozen grocery bags. I filled them with leaves and with the moist, fragrant compost from the bilge. Time passed too quickly. It was getting dark.

"I have to park it in front of the house for the night," I said.

It would be easier to clean out on the street. I could run a hose to it out there.

"I don't think that you should," Jennifer said. "You might get arrested. On second thought, park it out there and take your chances."

Jennifer had wandered back and forth from the house to the alley a half-dozen times. Keven was alongside her, like a trainer walking along with a fighter.

"You're not worried about theft?" I said, knowing what her answer would be.

"Ha!"

I cleared all bystanders out of the way and drove around to the front of the house, pretending I was a trucker with a wide load. Gordy Palzer and Joey the Actor and the Kallas boys, Endel and Eric, crossed the street for a look, all of them intrigued by the shape, the mysterious hulk in the city shadows. He was called Joey the Actor because he once worked as an extra in a crowd scene during the filming of a commercial for a Mexican fast-food restaurant chain—Joey the Actor, a little tuft of gray hair in the back of the crowd in a television commercial.

"A yacht," Joey the Actor said, being dramatic, "a yacht in our neighborhood. Just think."

Later, when other people saw the boat, some of them had memories of riding in such a boat when they were younger, but their memories didn't go deep enough to trigger more than polite curiosity. The men were on my side, though. Women were comforting Jennifer, telling her she was a saint.

"You girls might want to sing a little different tune when this baby is the queen of the lake," I said, "and you could be lounging in it, catching the sun like bathing beauties."

"It will never float," Jennifer said.

"Look at the faces on these guys," I said, indicating my neighbors. "Is that envy, or is that envy?"

Mostly, Gordy and Joey the Actor and the Kallas boys, Endel and Eric, looked happy that the boat wasn't theirs.

At last I bent down to disconnect the trailer from the car. Jennifer, Andy, and Emily stood on the dewy grass of the boulevard, three silhouettes. It was almost full dark.

"Holy shit!" I said.

"What?" The voices came from the boulevard.

"There's no coupling device on this trailer," I said. "The tongue of the trailer is just sitting on the ball."

"You mean," Jennifer said, "that you drove home like that?" She moved closer to Andy and put her arm around him.

I was too embarrassed to look up, knowing that those sharp hazel eyes of hers could drill me even in the dark.

"Yeah, and at the speed limit, too," I said. "Jesus H. Christ."

I thought back. I hadn't been watching. I was climbing around in the boat when Menth hooked it up. All he had done to secure the trailer to the car was to drop the trailer onto the ball and then wrap a tow chain around the tongue and the hitch, in the manner of a Hollywood cowboy tying the reins of his horse to a split rail with two quick wraps. We were lucky to have arrived home without an accident, but then it was probably the same way Menth had towed it back from Chaska.

A seventeen-foot Chris Craft Deluxe utility shipped out of Algonac, Michigan, in the fall of 1937 weighed 1,750 pounds.

We didn't tow that boat home so much as got chased by it.

4

WHY OLD MOTORBOATS evoke such distant and pleasant memories among their fanciers is no more a mystery, I suspect, than why attics do the same to the curious souls who explore them during summer thunderstorms, or why a collage of photographs in a grandmother's front room can seem suddenly to come to life with remembered people, how they looked and sounded and moved. Shapes and shadows and smells always conspire to drag susceptible souls back in time, so that the bonnet in the attic makes a young girl again of the mother who shyly models it for her children.

A utility boat in the slip, boxy and anachronistic, calls to mind endless summers and makes a boy again of the young man who resurrects one.

It was my father's boat hulking out there in the garage.

More accurately, it was precisely the same model, year, and make of the boat he had when I was a boy. Now I was putting myself into the old snapshots. I don't think that is an uncommon phenomenon. Young men sometimes have brief glimpses of themselves in the image of their fathers, in dealing with a child or signing a check or manipulating a cigarette or having a drink.

Boats turn on the time machine for me only because my father and I spent a great deal of time in boats. Sometimes when I thought about it just that way—"my father's boat"—I felt curiously entrusted with the keys to a fantastic kingdom of memory, and possibly more. Now that I was in my thirties, I had developed the notion that boats were introduced by one or the both of us at critical points in our lives to mediate our unspoken emotional relationship, that it was mysteriously easier for us to communicate feelings around the hull of an old boat, as though it were a conference table or a confessional, than it was to deal with each other more directly. Boats connected us; to have my father's precise boat, or its proximity, sharpened the connection, specifically at a time in life when such connections are just as easily neglected.

Bud's precise boat was thought to be lost or long since disintegrated, if there was a distinction. I imagined there was. I imagined that I would find his boat, dry, covered, in a barn in a grove of trees. There are apocryphal stories for every generation, of Dusenbergs found in the cobwebs of a widow's garage, of coins found in the wall spaces of renovated homes, of perfectly preserved turn-of-the-century newspapers found wedged under the sills of third-story windows.

My father gave his boat to Johnson Boat Works on the west shore of White Bear Lake at the end of the summer of 1962 to settle a ninety-dollar gasoline and storage bill. He laughed at the story years later, pointing out that it was a common enough way to dispose of a boat, especially one that was then twenty-five years old.

"It was just our boat," he would say, trying to make

me understand. I felt suddenly embarrassed that he might have thought my curiosity so needlessly sentimental. "Why," he said, "there was no more reason to keep that boat than you might have to keep the car you are driving at the moment."

His capacity to dismiss the past was boundless. He simply demonstrated no interest in revealing himself, which was maddening in its way, but a fact of his life. To my disappointment, he once gave away a drawerful of memorabilia from the St. Paul Winter Carnival, a pageant that is as curiously unique to St. Paul as the Mardi Gras is to New Orleans. The carnival was created by railroad and lumber barons before the turn of the century to convince wary easterners that even during the extremes of January, St. Paul was tolerable, so long as everyone rallied around an ice palace or went gliding around skating rinks illuminated by torches that flickered at the hard black sky.

I remember that one of the drawers behind his sliding closet door—there was a warren of shelves and drawers behind the closet doors in our parents' room—was full of carnival buttons, coins of the King Boreas realm, dinner programs, and ribbons. Much of it was from the year 1960, when he was one of the mysterious scarlet-coated Vulcans, but just as much was from earlier years, going back to the 1940s, when hundreds of marching units would fill the streets during the Grande Day Parade and the Vulcans would appear unannounced in the streets, sometimes after sneaking through the city's network of sewer tunnels.

He gave his carnival paraphernalia away, not remembering to whom and not expressing any particular regret that I would have been interested in caretaking it. I would have been. I remember the evening in 1960 when we drove him downtown and dropped him off with a suitcase in front of the St. Paul Athletic Club. We children wondered where he was going, but the Vulcans, like Laurel and Hardy's Sons of the Desert, were ridiculously secretive in accordance with the rules of the Royal Order of Fire and Brimstone.

"Where's Dad going?" we asked our mother after he had gotten out of the car and she had slid over to take the wheel.

"To Chicago," my mother said, with her mouth set in a line of disapproval, "on a business trip."

As I remember that night, that moment of departure in the cold in front of the club, I remember that she managed to make it sound like, "on a business trip, my ass." She was six months pregnant with my youngest sister. It is inconceivable to me now that I could go off to be a Vulcan for ten days and not tell my children. In fact, my children would demand to know—and they would get an answer.

As a Vulcan, one of a "krewe" of eight whose identities were kept secret through the ten days of the carnival, he stormed around the town clinging to the back of an antique fire truck, alighting here and there, cape flying, to run down the shrieking females of St. Paul and smudge their faces with soot, the mark of Vulcan. The eight were, by name, Grand Duke Fertilius, Prince of Soot, Count of Ashes, Baron Hot Sparkus, Count Embrious, General Flamous, Duke of Klinker, and their leader, Vulcanus Rex.

Our father was the Duke of Klinker.

Even though we weren't supposed to know that he was a Vulcan, we dragged it out of our mother, who uncharacteristically kept studying the 6 P.M. newscasts every night during carnival week. Then, along with her, we watched the news every night for film clips of the carnival in which the Vulcans were sometimes background figures, racing by in their truck or coming comically out of the revolving doors of a department store, shooting blanks into the cold, gray air. Hail Vulcan! By legend, the Vulcans, after ten days of raising hell, would dethrone King Boreas in a torchlight uprising that symbolically put an end to winter.

Hell, yes, I would have been interested in the treasures of that drawer. At times I can imagine what he must have been like as a Vulcan—sly, definitely sly behind greasepaint and robes. At other times it strikes me as incredible that he could have placed himself in such a theatrical position. He was too impossibly well mannered. And yet, he told me once that during his ten-day stint he had been given a key to the steam room of the St. Paul Athletic Club so that he could go up there at two in the morning to sweat out the poison, smiling conspiratorially at the memory, wondering how he had survived it all. At the time he was forty-two years old, heavy, a smoker, and never one to shy away at the cocktail hour.

I didn't press him on the squandered utility boat, having learned in the course of my life not to press him on much, for he evidently suspected that nostalgia was indicative of emotional sensationalism. I tried to get him going a number of times about his role in India in World War II. My curiosity was inspired by the discovery in his special closet space of black-and-white photographs of Indian funeral pyres built on the banks of a wide and muddy river. There were other pictures, too, of Indian men sitting on Calcutta streets, the legs of the men terribly bloated and presumably infected. In one picture an Indian looks into the camera lens, his enormous eyes shy under the soiled cloth wrap around his forehead.

There was so much I didn't know about my father. All of what I didn't know seemed to square so solidly against the evidence of such an entirely normal childhood that I yearned to know more. Maybe the boat in my garage would open the door to more knowledge about him.

Children invariably express more curiosity about their fathers. Mothers, especially of my mother's generation, were not so disinclined to talk, reminisce, and tell stories about themselves. For the most part, mothers of my mother's generation were at home, available. While my father's secrets were kept in a drawer, or in his very being, my mother's were out in the open, in her natural gabbiness, in pictures of her parents, brothers, and sisters, flattened under the heavy glass of her dressing table.

I know that my mother's favorite sandwich as a girl was buttered bread sprinkled with sugar. Later, as a working woman, she had a chicken salad sandwich and a chocolate shake every day at the lunch counter where she eventually met Bud. Mothers are full of information, much of it confessional in nature. Mothers are open books. Men— fathers—are not, at least not in the snapshot years that fascinate me. Not that it's terribly critical to anything, but I couldn't tell you for the life of me what my father used to eat for lunch.

During the "beer-town" World Series between Milwaukee and St. Louis in 1982, I idled away the day of game six by driving from my hotel in downtown St. Louis to Alton, Illinois, to see the house where my mother was born and raised. In my mental image of the place, I had always imagined Alton to be directly across the river from St. Louis, not upriver as I discovered.

If ever there was a town worthy of mystery and intrigue, it was Alton, an old river town; my mother had a connection to water, too. I felt as though I knew the place and could see my mother and her brothers and sisters going up and down the hills in an open car trying to get cool on hot, muggy summer nights, their father, my grandfather, with a stub of unlit cigar between his teeth. He was a

Democrat, John McHale was, but so violently opposed to Roosevelt's New Deal that his children believed that the high blood pressure that killed their father at fifty-six was directly communicated to Alton from the White House. John McHale didn't begin a day without throwing down the newspaper and crying out, "that goddamn Roosevelt!"

Alton was old when I saw it on that cool, overcast morning in mid-October. Its homes and businesses listed painfully toward the Mississippi; it was a river town, putting me instantly in mind of Huck and Pap. I could easily picture my mother there, in the tall, angular, Victorian-style home on Liberty Street. I could hear her laughter and the laughter of her brothers and sisters, a mirthful, uproarious crew of seven. They are teachers, hospital administrators, book publishers, and iconoclasts now, one of whom was guaranteed, in any gathering, to tell of the visit to their home of Al Ernst. Ernst, a friend of John McHale, was a salesman who traveled with a trunk full of potions and elixirs for his extraordinary hypochondria. Through his poorly fitting false teeth he was inspired to tell the McHale children: "When you got chur hellsh, you gotch everyshing."

Other boats followed that Chris Craft utility. In our house, boats, to use my father's analogy, were as common as automobiles, and just as practically used in our pursuits and recreations. Not expensive boats, mind you, not even sleek ones, but serviceable. We were fortunate enough to have been raised on water, a blessing descended from my father's father, whom, like John McHale, I never knew. Henry Soucheray established the property at White Bear in 1904, building a cottage surrounded on three sides by a screen porch on the east shore of White Bear Lake in the village of Mahtomedi.

The village was a classic: one rail depot, one store, one gas station, and one saloon, Vince Guarnera's tavern at the top of Juniper Street. My visits to Guarnera's were illicit, connected invariably to my tagging along with Bud when he drove out from town in the fall to check on the utility boat.

I remember one of those autumn days vividly. It was late on a Saturday afternoon, deep into the Eisenhower administration. We walked around the side of the cottage next to the swamp, my father pushing aside the long willow branches that streaked the windows of the cottage and left rusting yellow leaves on the dirt path next to the swamp, the low spot of land where the rain gathered in brackish green pools and tall grasses and cattails grew. It must have been how the land around the lake looked hundreds of years past when the Sioux and Dakota Indians camped there. *Mahtomedi* was Sioux for "White Bear."

The cottage sat on a bump of land in a long, narrow yard, the yard soft and velvety with long grass. The yard was thick with acorns in the fall. The yard sloped to a rampart at the beach, a stone wall running across the front of the yard. It was two wood steps down to the sand and rocks and the water rolling in, smelling fragrantly of fish. Leaf smoke lay over the water. Gulls were assembled out in the middle of the lake in dark, irregular clusters. The sitting gulls squawked at the ones taking flight, the whiteness of the flying ones metallic between the still sky and the slate-colored water.

We were alone that day except for the gulls out there under the streamers of smoke. Most of the docks up and down the shoreline had been brought in, but ours still made a gray line of weathered boards straight out into the lake. The platform that made the T at the end of the dock had been disassembled and stacked up on shore, but so long as the Chris Craft still hung on its hoist, there was dock enough to get to it. The boat made a shadow of itself on the glassy water under the bronze-colored bottom; we had come out from town to drain the bilge after a week of autumn rain.

At the foot of the dock we stopped, and my father put his hand out to keep me from passing him.

"Judas Priest," he said. That was as low as his language ever dropped in front of children. Once, driving by the White Bear Yacht Club, I saw a funnel cloud forming over the eighteenth hole. I saw it out of the passenger window of the car.

"Hey, Dad, what's that?" I said.

He bent over the dash to look up at the sky.

"Judas Priest!"

Now he was saying it again, incensed and anxious.

"Look," he said, "the windshield is broken. Look out there."

I looked around him. The boat was facing shore, hanging on its ancient apparatus of timbers that resembled a gallows. The square-cornered windshield was shattered with a spidery wound.

"Kids with rocks, I'll bet," he said.

We walked out to the boat, the water clean in the shadow made by the dock. The stone was in the front seat of the boat. Bud climbed in, rocking the boat as he did so, and then he took my hand and helped me climb in after him. The boat swung free on its lifting rings after the exertion of our entering it, the strain of the swinging making the sound of an unoiled porch swing. Bud tossed out the rock. Then he reached down into the bilge under the front seat, found the brass drain plug, and unscrewed it. We heard the water spilling out below us as we sat on the covering boards to tilt the boat and speed up the drainage. Water with a faint rainbow swirl of oil and gas drifted out from under the hull.

The boat was then twenty years old but common enough, serviceable, seaworthy for even the roughest chop that White Bear could stir up. Sixty horses was plenty in a seventeen-foot boat, four cylinders that distinguished themselves with a pleasant chugging and gurgling out the exhaust pipe. Man has yet to make music any sweeter than the sound of such an engine at low speed. The specific sweetness of the sound—the gurgling, followed by a pause, as though to catch a breath, followed by the gurgling again— was the result of the engine discarding water through an exhaust system that had a dip and a bend built into it, creating chambers where sound formed.

The entire boat was mahogany, so instantly and universally recognizable that it might have inspired the artists of children's books when they were called upon to illustrate a motorboat. The blue upholstery was dulled from years in the sun and rain, same with the light-blue linoleum floor. The hardware had lost its brightness. On the two or three occasions when Johnson Boat Works refinished it, my father swore that they substituted brown paint for the more original red-tinted filler stain that gave the mahogany its luster.

The interior siding was olive-colored, drab, possibly as the result of the same refinishing crew across the lake not wishing to stain and varnish the interior. The deck seams, though straight and white when new, had accumulated deposits of yellowed varnish over the years. The deteriorating condition of the boat sometimes exasperated my father, and at other times he seemed cheerfully resolved that he would never have a piece of equipment that he could keep free from the unintentional ruin of time, not to mention children.

What remained distinguished and proud-looking on that boat was the instrument panel. It was oval-shaped, encompassing a revolutions-per-minute gauge, oil pressure gauge, and ammeter. Each instrument had white lettering on a black face, with thin, fragile, white needles that pulsed when the glass over the instruments was tapped with a finger. The instruments were fit into a stamped plate etched with speedboats racing around buoys on the Detroit River.

The brisk, refreshing air advertised the change of seasons. To this day any similar feeling in the air tightens the muscles deep in my stomach, and I think back to that day, the two of us in that boat, in silence and the presence of water that we loved, my father's contentment, his very posture of ease seeming to say to me, "You could do worse than to aspire to similar moments yourself someday."

"We'll have to take it to Johnson's no later than next week," my father said. "Winter's coming." He brushed beads of water off the engine house with his bare hand and lifted the engine cover to have a look at the motor. Lifting the hatch released the perfume of the bilge.

"Might as well leave the drain plug out," he said.

He climbed out first and then helped me onto the dock. He looked out at the gulls and then up and down the shoreline, and I did the same. Walking off the dock he speculated about the busted windshield, mostly to himself, and mumbled something about having a new piece of glass cut in town and then having Buster Johnson across the lake install it next spring.

We checked the cottage on our way out to the car, walking through its dark, stale rooms. The striped canvas awnings were down on three sides of the porch. Already the cold air was getting trapped in the cottage for the long winter when we would not be driving out. Our time with the cottage was coming to an end, its era passing, making way for the new. That very fall my father had pulled the longer of two straws out of a glass and beat my uncle Phil out of the lakeshore property. My father had hired Homer Jensen to build a year-round home on the site of the cottage, the home where I was raised, rooms with expansive glass looking out at the water. The breakwater, the rampart, came down in the building process, but an oak tree at the corner of the front yard remained, an oak tree of the ages, still there to this day.

We had one more stop to make that day, Vince Guarnera's saloon, white-sided with a green-shingled roof, at the top of the hill on Juniper Street where it intersected the main village road. It was dark inside and warm. The saloon was filled with the murmurings of the men who lived in Mahtomedi year-round. It smelled good. Beer and Italian food. The food smells came through the open door to the kitchen in the back, a glimpse of a white porcelain stove back there with claw feet sinking into the wood floor. We came in from crisp air to the warm embrace of tobacco smoke. When we came through the door Vince walked to the end of the bar nearest the front door. His black hair was brilliant, and the closely shaved sides of his head were shiny in the off-light of the saloon. Behind the bar was a grotto of color made by an opening where the bottles had been pushed aside for a Hamm's Beer display, showing a deep blue lake, the land of sky-blue waters. Around the shore of the lake were pines, the deep blue of the lake and dark green of the pines as sharp as Christmas bulbs in the darkness. At that age, I always thought the lake was White Bear.

"Hello, Henry," Vince said in a husky voice.

"Hello, Vince."

Vince put a glass of Hamm's in front of my father, a Coke for me. I climbed up on the stool beside him, invigorated by being in a place of such sharp colors and low talk and the metallic ringing of the pinball machine in the back.

"Another, Henry?" My father was smoking a Lucky, but holding it like a German commandant might, the stream of smoke drifting away from his fingers.

"Well, now that you mention it, Vince."

But another was the last. We had the long drive ahead of us. On days such as those, as young as I was, I sensed the finality of another summer having drawn to a close.

5

OLD BOATS MIGHT NEVER HAVE BECOME my passion, my obsession, my hobby of relentless emotional adventuring, except that I attended, in 1976, the first-ever Antique and Classic Boat Rendezvous at Lake Minnetonka. Lake Minnetonka, to anyone in Minnesota even remotely charmed by motorboats, is the mother lake, the lode. Large, scenic, it is surrounded by mile after mile of extraordinary homes, many of them built on channels and inlets and bays and backwaters. It's as close as we in Minnesota will get to Annapolis and its neighboring Eastern Shore or the Finger Lakes region of New York or the cabin country in Ontario.

Minnetonka has history, a history of large resort hotels and of unique streetcar service from Minneapolis and St. Paul to Excelsior, where streetcar boats, patterned in shape and color after the electric cars, departed for the picnic grounds on Big Island. There were six streetcar boats, *The Como*, *The Harriet*, *The Hopkins*, *The Minnehaha*, *The Stillwater*, and *The White Bear*, each of them as boxy and as fantailed as the cars on land. One of them, the cyprus-hulled *Minnehaha,* was salvaged in the summer of 1980. It was brought to the surface off Big Island, where it had been scuttled in 1926. It came up rolled on its side, as ghostly and bleached as a pirate brig.

Another of the streetcar boats, *The Minnetonka,* was scuttled intact, complete with its pilot house, benches, railings, hardware, and engines, and is still down there somewhere in seventy feet of murky water. It is haunting to think of the old tubs down there, on any lake. Bud often spoke of a sunken ferryboat on White Bear, sunk between the peninsula and Manitou Island. In the 1920s ferryboats and, later, speedboats ran passenger rides from Wildwood Amusement Park in Wildwood Bay on the deep southeast corner of White Bear.

A notice of that first antique and classic boat show at Minnetonka caught my eye—startled me, really—and made me suddenly think of boats. After twenty years of lake life, I had spent fifteen years dry-docked, with school and marriage and children and newspapering—all city-based. Against the odds of my watery background I had become a sportswriter, once having had to admit to my colleagues that the first professional baseball game I covered as a reporter was the second game I had ever seen in person. I simply had forgotten, or unwittingly set aside over the intervening years on dry land, the monumental role that boats had played in my upbringing. Boats and water. The day John F. Kennedy was shot? There was mist like a shroud over White Bear, the lake not yet frozen in late November 1963. I was on the lake the day man set foot on the moon in July 1969. During race riots in Detroit and Los Angeles, during Vietnam, during Chicago '68, during hell and high water, I was on the lake.

Enthusiasts, most of whom lived on or around Lake Minnetonka, had assembled among them enough antique and classic Chris Crafts, Centuries, Hackers, and Gar Woods to develop a regional "Land O' Lakes" chapter of the Antique and Classic Boat Society of North America, formed just two years earlier. I didn't know it then, but I was walking in on the ground floor of the antique boat movement, at least in Minnesota. The aspiring Land O' Lakes people used the docks of what was then the most fashionable of the lakeside Minnetonka restaurants, Lord Fletchers. The restaurant was built on channel water, the number of channels on that lake never ceasing to amaze and intrigue me. Minnetonka was three times as big as White Bear, each lake anchoring its twin city: Minnetonka for Minneapolis, White Bear for St. Paul.

Lord Fletchers had docks on the narrow channel, with a patio overlooking the docks. Girls working on tans worked on the docks, tying up the arriving boats; on summer weekends the boats and the people around Lord Fletchers made a rich pageantry of color, glistening skin coated with tanning butter. There was a volleyball sandpit and Campari umbrella tables, with expensive glass boats waterside and BMWs and Porsches by land.

Into this high-tech, pre-Yuppie scene on an August weekend in 1976 came the antique boaters, as quaint as scouts in knee-high socks.

The show began on Saturday morning and that first year featured mostly Chris Crafts, but also a Larson and a Dunphy. There had been a Chris Craft in our family as recently as 1968, the "Chris Craft That Broke Loose from the Car." I thought about that boat and then I thought about the utility boat. The squandered utility, turned over to settle an account was the story I had always heard.

"Ninety bucks!" I said when I saw my father out at White Bear a week or so after the show. "Do you know what that thing would be worth today?"

I was full of new expertise as I told him about the show.

"Junk," he said of his old utility.

"No way, not at all," I said. "Old boats are the rage; it's a cult thing or something. Old boats are making a comeback, as collector's items."

"Ah," he said. He waved his hand, dismissing me, and laughed, not unkindly, but in a way that implied I was wasting my time.

"You really should go to that show next year," I told him. "You'd love it."

I didn't wait for the next show to come around. I wandered the grounds of that first show so slack-jawed and so vulnerable to sentiment and nostalgia that I joined the fledgling national organization before I ever left the grounds. Over the winter I began receiving the first of countless newsletters. I also started looking for a boat. I didn't make my newfound passion very public within the walls of my own home, incidentally. My passion started slowly, secretively. Those boat club newsletters became as anxiously anticipated as the next message on a secret decoder ring.

I didn't find a boat. My father did. We were riding on his pontoon boat the next summer, in 1977, when he took care to point out a twenty-two-foot Chris Craft Sportsman tied to a dock down on the east shore of the lake. The boat looked rough. He nosed his pontoon in close, and we looked it over, wondering if it might be for sale. It was low in the water. It was identical to the boat that he had acquired when he willed away the old utility. It was a boat we had owned during my teenage years; if my younger brothers and sisters were as much inclined toward sentiment as I am, this boat would provide the same sentimental awakenings for them as the utility had done for me. We were, that summer, going on nine years without a wood boat in the family.

"Who owns this sad-looking baby?" I asked Bud.

The pontoon was full of passengers engaged in their own conversations, so our communication had the appearance of two people trying to arrange dinner plans over a crowd at a subway platform. He did not know who owned it at the moment, he said over the shoulder of a grandchild, but he reminded me of its previous owners. It was a boat that he knew.

"I'll find out," I said.

We motored away, his attention returning to the gathering at hand, his children, daughters-in-law, sons-in-law, grandchildren. My eyes stayed focused on the boat. That brief glimpse of the boat, its possibly being for sale, and our even-briefer conversation about it stirred something deep inside me. I am not sure what. It struck me at that moment that there was that time and there was before and there was a gap in the middle. I am not even sure it was a gap that needed to be filled, or that it constituted a problem that needed to be defined. But the boat was the genesis of the stirring.

It didn't take but a week of modest sleuthing to produce the owner, whose name is impossible to forget: Billy Joe House, maybe twenty years old, tops. I knocked on the door that seemed most directly up from the dock where the boat was lashed, was directed to a house farther back from the lake, knocked there, and Billy Joe House answered the door, pulling up his jeans as he did so. I had awakened him. I told him I would like to buy his boat. I don't think the thought of selling had occurred to him, but I had purposely caught him at a time of the year when he might have realized that any day now he would be responsible for getting a 2,000-pound boat out of the lake and storing it, an inconvenient task under the best of circumstances.

Billy Joe House didn't look like he had any circumstances. He looked like a college kid who had lived on the water for a summer, had stumbled into the ownership of an old boat, and might now be ripe for the picking.

"Eight hundred dollars," House said, yawning.

"Two hundred," I said, wondering if he would invite me in.

"Six hundred," House said, his eyes focusing, warming up to the prospect of money.

"Four hundred," I said.

"Four hundred fifty," he said.

"Sold," I said, reaching for my checkbook before he changed his mind.

It really was that simple. Then again, I hadn't exactly purchased a Barnes or a LaCalle or a Ditchburn, the exotic, rare wines of antique boating. The Chris Craft Sportsman was possibly the most common boat ever built for the average American boater. Collectors generally pass on the Sportsman model and concentrate their searches for more-limited production models, such as postwar nineteen-foot racing runabouts, of which only 503 were ever built, or Rivieras or hydroplanes, or twin-engined Continentals. Thousands of Sportsmen were built. The Sportsman, incidentally, had a starring role in the movie *On Golden Pond*, which did more than any other event in world history to familiarize people with antique and classic boats; there were always three or four Sportsmen in the Minnetonka shows, shown by Minnetonka people who still had them in use as everyday boats.

The exact date of the transaction was September 23, 1977. For some reason I was compelled to make notes. The weather was humid, with overcast skies, a little moaning wind out of the south. I wrote Billy Joe House a check and walked down to take possession. The boat was awash—that is, it was sitting on the bottom, full of rainwater and neglect. It obviously leaked. Cushions and seat backs were floating, but they were too waterlogged to float above the confining perimeters of the boat. I was not even party to bringing the boat back down the shore to Bud's. He and my brother Paul and a brother-in-law or two pumped the boat out a few days later and then towed it back down the shoreline.

Minor logistical problems were easily solved. I could not keep the boat at my house in St. Paul. I did not have a garage deep enough. It would have to remain at the lake, in the available third stall of Bud's garage. Bud was agreeable; my mother was not. She feared for the safety of Paul, the youngest of us, who was then only eleven. She was convinced, however illogically, that once trailered and in the garage the Sportsman would somehow shift around on its own and tip over on top of Paul, her baby.

"Mom, these things weigh more than your house," I told her. "It's not going anywhere."

The Billy Joe House Sportsman sat in the garage for seven years, getting only refinished, not restored, during all of that time. The commuting alone, from my house in town out to the lake, is what convinced me to acquire a seventeen-foot boat, one that would fit in my garage, at my house, in my town.

We finally launched that Sportsman in June of 1983, using it infrequently, for it was frequently unreliable, and selling it in May 1984. Those seven years were instructive, even if only for getting my hands on the wood, figuring out how far I should go into a disassembly, exploring the boat's fragrant mysteries. The boat shows became an annual ritual for us—me, my father, my son, my brothers and brothers-in-law. Every summer we'd go to the show, congratulating ourselves that our Sportsman was destined to be a show winner. We associated the ridiculous amount of time we spent on it with the precision of our workmanship, which really wasn't workmanship but procrastination.

Not until 1980, the summer when there was a buzzing of excitement among lake people about the raising of one of the streetcar boats, did a seventeen-foot square-windshield utility show up at the rendezvous. It was Menth's. Me and Andy and Bud and Paul were drawn to it through the crowds on the dock, having gotten just a glimpse of it from afar. By 1980 the show had outgrown the available slips at Lord Fletchers and had moved to the network of docks in front of adjoining restaurants in Excelsior, on the site of what once had been the Excelsior Amusement Park. The shows were beginning to attract fifty to seventy-five boats by 1980.

We were drawn to Menth's slip and stood around it speechless, watching Menth, whom we did not then know, polishing the bright work and wiping splashed water from the deck that glistened deep into the ages of memory. He had a red flannel blanket folded like a lap robe over the back of the front seat, the seat upholstered in green leather.

Menth couldn't help but acknowledge us. We stood there like dolts, with our mouths open. At least Bud and I did, me looking at Bud and then back to the boat again, in a mixture of delight and disbelief.

"This is the one, isn't it?" I said. "This is it!"

I nudged the old man. I said, "Jesus, man, this is your boat." And he said, "I'll be damned," and then I said, "Ninety bucks. Nice. Ninety dollars. You gave away one like this." And then I explained to Andy that this was the one, and Paul, in the middle, had it explained to him by Bud.

Menth, during all this time, stared up at us, his hand shielding his eyes from the glare of the summer sun.

"We had a boat like this," my father explained for me, bringing Menth into it at last.

"When I was his age," I said, putting my arm around Andy's shoulders.

Aside from the instantly awakened memories, I was taken with the boat's design, its lines, how nifty it was, how perfect, clean, and buoyant. How much I had forgotten and how much I was suddenly remembering.

"Would you fellas like a ride?" Menth said. They were his first words.

We lowered ourselves off the high dock into the boat. I sat on the engine box; Bud, Andy, and Paul were in the backseat, grinning for my camera. Menth sat on the covering board, steering easily with one hand on the wheel, his head turned toward us, saying, "Brings back memories, does it?"

He taxied us around the boat show docks. I didn't want the ride to end.

6

$\wedge\wedge\wedge\wedge\wedge\wedge\wedge\wedge\wedge\wedge\wedge\wedge\wedge\wedge$

DURING THE FIRST FEW DAYS the boat was home, in the sultriest summer days of 1984, I didn't think I could handle the responsibility of such a demanding project. After the comedy of its arrival wore thin and the neighbors and other curious souls had wandered back to the activities of normal, productive lives, there I remained, the fool on the block, beginning to get parted from his senses and soon enough from his money.

The boat was undeniably weather-beaten, with serious structural dry rot, and yet the hull, by my amateur understanding of it, was entirely restorable. For example, although two starboard side planks were rotted near the stern (easily patched with old scrap mahogany), the hull planking in general was surprisingly sound, and probably, as a result of it being so uniformly weathered, far more luxurious-looking and deeply golden colored upon completion than new stock lumber.

I cleaned the leaves, mouse turds, and acorns out of

the bilge with a toy shovel from the sandbox, a cleaning process that was an extension of what I had begun the first night the boat was home. For more thorough cleaning, I jacked up the nose of the trailer and then, using a garden hose with a nozzle, flushed soapy water straight out the stern where I had already removed the bottommost transom plank. I slapped that board in a gesture intended to demonstrate the boat's soundness and the board fell into the street. Unlike the side planking, the stern planking needed replacement. Imagine buying an old house and then discovering that it was so totally in disrepair that when you went to scrub what was left of the kitchen floor you also knocked out a wall of the house so that the wash water had someplace to drain.

I needed help. I had set certain imperatives in place; I had the makings of the boat I wanted. It fit in my garage. It was precisely Bud's boat, or as close to his as I thought I would ever get.

But I needed help. I didn't want to discuss it very much with Jennifer, not wanting to give her a chance to say I told you so or to give her the idea that I anticipated having to spend money that we hadn't necessarily intended to spend on a boat. What I told her was how nifty it would be if only I could run into a carpenter who had a little spare time on his hands.

"A retired guy," I said.

"What about Ray?" Jennifer said one day, about three weeks after the boat had been brought home.

Just his name struck so suddenly at the heart of things that I heard choirs singing.

"Ray!"

Jennifer had had the answer all along; she just made me sweat for it. I don't know why Ray didn't occur to me, although I might have unconsciously dismissed him on the grounds that to my knowledge he had never even seen a Chris Craft, much less worked on one.

Ray Stawikoski was one of a fading breed of American man—thick-wristed, pleasantly thick-headed, the kind of guy who looked perfect in the khaki twill work pants from Sears Roebuck. He knew how to build things. From tongue depressors he made wooden sculptures that twirled like windmills. He could take a Coke can and a tin snips and end up with a biplane, complete with spinning, pinwheel propeller. He was a lifelong pattern maker who had become friends with Jennifer's father when the two of them began using the same charter service to fly to gambling vacations in Las Vegas. It is a curious way to know a man when he is a friend of your father-in-law. That is about as far out on the perimeter of familiarity as you can get, except that Jennifer's people have a remarkable skill for pulling people in from the rim and making them seen as recognizable as your own aunts or uncles. Years earlier, for Christmas, Ray had built a cradle for Emily's dolls on commission for my mother-in-law. He might as well have been a boat builder now that I thought about it. He countersunk his screws and plugged his holes with bungs. He glued and screwed. He was an extraordinarily careful and elaborate builder.

It wasn't long before Ray was occasionally at our house, building a flower box, repairing a railing, or building a set of built-in bookshelves that were so sturdy that Ray stood up on the shelves and bounced up and down when he was done installing them. Those shelves marked an adult rite of passage for my generation, incidentally—the leap from the sagging-pine-planks-across-bricks stage of life into the stage of level book display, their jackets finally lined up properly across a wall.

So, yes: Ray. When Jennifer mentioned his name I knew instantly that there wouldn't be a piece of that boat that he couldn't reproduce. He came from a generation of workmen, not unlike the workmen in Algonac, Michigan, building Chris Crafts, who did what had to be done and did not wait to do it. Besides, he was retired. And I needed a pattern maker. The first few weeks of disassembly revealed considerable structural deterioration. The transom, where I first started poking around, had rotted away behind the scenes. Not only did the visible stern planking need replacement, but the port and starboard transom cheeks—the interior vertical braces at each corner of the stern—had to be replaced as well.

Rotted pieces of the chine, the beautifully curved piece of oak that forms the perimeter design of the boat at the juncture of the sides and the bottom, had to be cut away, with new pieces sistered in to replace the old. The stakes, vertical pieces standing from under the rear deck to the stern chine, were bad. The transom battens were bad. I was intrigued with the word *batten*, pleased to understand a new definition. Back in the days when I raced sailboats, I understood battens to be the three thin strips of wood in graduated lengths that I inserted into the mainsail to stiffen the trailing edge of the sail. Battens in a motorboat are thin strips of oak behind the line where two side planks, or two deck planks, meet each other. The saying "batten down the hatches" suddenly made sense to me—nailing down a strip of wood to overlap both hatch covers so they couldn't bang open in a storm.

Some boat restorers and collectors belittle the Chris Craft by suggesting that they might as well have been built in high school shop classes, compared with the more intricate and finely crafted Hacker Crafts or some of the Canadian boats, the Greavette and the Ditchburn. Chris Crafts were crafted well enough, and complicated enough, for me. I was astonished at the complexity of that looming hull, that hulk in my garage, especially down low in the bilge and in the strange, distant lands under the front and rear decks, where, as a boy, I had been afraid to poke my head.

I tried explaining some of this to Ray on the telephone.

"Gee, Joe," Ray said, "I don't know anything about boats."

"But you know about wood."

"Well, yes."

"How about if you take a look at it."

Ray knew that I didn't know much about woodworking. He must have picked that up from being around me during his shelf-building. I probably inspired him with a story or two for around his poker table.

"The H of it is," Ray said, "I don't know when I'd find the time."

I suppose that I was five weeks into it before Ray saw the boat. I'm not sure he knew what he was looking at. I had so thoroughly stripped it first of its jewelry and then of its wood components that it looked roughly like a boat, but a boat without a back end and no innards. It looked like a sun-bleached, scrapped hull, like something once seaworthy but now washed up on the sand in a *National Geographic* photo essay.

Ray physically shied away from it. He wouldn't stand next to it. He stood a few paces away, looking at it from under the visor of his cap. I told him why I wanted to restore that particular boat, that my father had had one just like it, that someday soon I wanted to take my father for a ride in it. Ray, too, I quickly added, although I'd bet a ride was the furthest thing from Ray's mind.

"If you want a boat like this, Ray," I tried to explain, condensing my eight or so years of hand-me-down knowledge, "you sometimes have to take them in this condition. I know it looks rough, but I've seen worse."

Ray was speechless. I am sure the wheels of his brain were spinning to get him out of the garage, back into the sunlight, then to the safety of his Plymouth station wagon, and then finally cross-town to his home. Then again, I am also certain that he felt some sort of obligation to his friend, my father-in-law, who, not so incidentally, occasionally let Ray use his lake cabin in northern Minnesota.

"Ray," I said, trying to snap him out of it, "believe me, I've seen them worse than this." Ray opened his mouth but no words came out.

In the summer of 1980, acting on a tip from our new friend Menth, my father, Andy, my brother Paul, and I had explored the sheds at Cochrane's, one of the oldest boat yards at Minnetonka. Cochrane's was visible from the boat show docks, across Excelsior Bay, and Menth pointed to it from his slip at the show. Not ten minutes after the conclusion of our ride in Menth's boat, we drove over there looking for a utility of our own. Back in the shadows of a tin-roofed shed, where the dirt floor was cool and powdery and the place smelled like mildew, was a Chris Craft utility. We thought it was a seventeen-footer, just what the sight of the Menth boat inspired us to be after. It had the correct flat windshield, too, but in the dark we couldn't tell much except the general design. We didn't act on it.

Two years later, one autumn Sunday, I responded to a classified ad for a seventeen-foot Chris Craft utility, located in the suburbs north of Minneapolis. I went out there and lo, behind a garage in a neatly trimmed yard, was the boat from the shadows of the Cochrane shed. It was not a seventeen-footer. It was, in fact, a 1935 eighteen-footer, as rare a boat as I've encountered, so charmingly narrow-beamed, it was almost canoelike. I bought it.

It had a rich aroma, that one, rotting wood, mice and muskrat scat, compost, deteriorating stuffing from an old life jacket, grease, oil, gasoline. But there was more. Its bilge offered up seventy-three cents in change that to me seemed virtually antique: a 1966 quarter, a 1976 quarter, a 1946 dime, a 1957 dime, and three pennies, 1945, 1964, 1967. The 1946 dime was so blackened from its years in the bilge that it looked purple-black. It left a delicate imprint when I picked it off the bottom, under where the front seat would have been.

The same boat produced a rusted Schmidt beer can opener, the church key kind now rarely seen in modern kitchens, a cork fishing bobber, spools of monofilament fishing line, a Lazy Ike lure with rusted treblehooks, and what I presumed to be a stick for measuring gas. It was a yardstick advertising a long-gone hardware store, with the store's telephone number listed in the old-style exchange: "Call Garden 6 XXXX for all your hardware needs."

I let that boat go, principally because it had a fiber-glassed bottom. There was no telling the strength of the wood under the fiberglass, although I had become reasonably certain that old boats ended up fiberglassed only in order to get a last gasp out of them. Also, at eighteen feet, it did not quite fit into the garage. I had it in the garage from corner to corner, not straight in. Once, when I was standing in the stern, the bow went up into the rafters of the garage, bringing the nose of the trailer with it, putting me on the low end of a 2,000-pound teeter-totter. I was afraid that if I moved my weight forward the boat and trailer would crash down hard on the concrete floor. I had to yell for help. Jennifer came out and couldn't see me, just the upended bow of the boat sticking into the rafters.

"Where are you?" she said.

"Here," I said, peeking over the side of the boat from the back, "you better get Chet."

And out came Chet, as laconic as usual. He gently lowered the tongue of the trailer back to the floor and held it there with his foot until I moved forward, and the boat stabilized.

I considered making a hole in the garage wall to accommodate the tongue of the trailer, but I thought better of such impulsive alterations. Jennifer might not have appreciated a trailer nosing itself through the garage and into the backyard.

Through a local marine dealer I stored that boat over the winter at the 4-H barn at the Minnesota state fairgrounds and then sold it directly out of the barn the next spring to an allergist whose means were more considerable than mine in the event he wanted to punch a hole in his garage. Last I heard, the allergist hauled the boat to his brother's place in Alexandria, Minnesota, where together they were going to attempt to restore it.

I learned from that boat. I learned that the one I was after was still out there. I learned to keep moving and keep shuffling and keep looking.

"That eighteen-footer was worse, Ray," I said. "Believe me, I've seen worse than this baby."

I didn't want to let Ray get away. To have my boat professionally restored would have cost a minimum of $15,000, assuming that I could have found a restorer who wouldn't try to talk me out of it.

Ray still wouldn't speak. I kept blabbering. I handed

him the starboard transom cheek. Not only was it rotted, but a hollow had been eaten out of the middle of it, probably by ants. For three weeks after I brought it home, big black carpenter ants kept appearing out of an opening they evidently had eaten for themselves just below the covering board, up near the front seat.

"I wouldn't want to put the new one in," he said. He was lightly hefting the cheek, turning it every which way, sighting down it, too.

"But you could make a piece like that?" It was peculiarly bent, a graceful piece of oak.

"I can make it," Ray said, "but you better put it back in." Ray was such a practical man that he might have feared some sort of claim against him in the event the boat ever broke apart one day. He couldn't seem to emphasize enough that he would make pieces but he didn't actually want to work on the hull itself.

"I'll put the pieces in, Ray, I'll do that," I said, already figuring out how I would manage it. "I've done other boats, Ray, but I only fixed them up when you get right down to it. I only refinished them. This one will take some real work, some carpentry and rebuilding, but I know it can be done."

Ray lapsed into silence again.

"Now, Ray, look at these pieces," I said. Maybe I would find a piece of wood that tricked him into movement or speech.

I showed him what I had discovered in the bilge, that each chine gusset was cracked, that for three or four feet forward of the stern the chine itself had begun to roll away— it was bowing out—out of exhaustion and age.

I hadn't even discovered the bad stem yet.

"Hand me one of those braces," Ray said, meaning a chine gusset. A chine gusset is shaped just like one of the missing pieces in a 10,000-piece jigsaw puzzle. I don't know how else to describe one—an upside-down pistol butt? Each gusset joins a side frame to a main floor frame. Evidently, they were susceptible to cracking, as a result of both age and the stress of the boat rolling in turbulent water. I had vivid boyhood memories of cracking sounds, some of them as sharp as a bat on a ball, deep in the bowels of the boat when we were out in big waves or crossing somebody's hard wake.

Now Ray had a cheek and a gusset in his hands. I showed him the rot in the king planks under the deck. "Those pieces are just pine, Ray," I said.

"You've got to save pieces," Ray said, stating his code. "Whenever I do something like this, and I've never done anything like this, I always save the old pieces. I can do anything as long as I can see what it is I'm supposed to make."

Ray reminded me of my grandmother Anna, Bud's mother, who had died ten years earlier at ninety-six. Anna saved everything—string, scraps of brown paper, envelopes, paperclips—but best of all, my uncle Phil's electrically illuminated diorama of ducks on the wing over a pond, tall grasses around the pond. The diorama was about as big as a dollhouse. She kept it in a spare bedroom, where, when it was lit in the darkened room, it cast a soft yellow October glow in the darkness, the miniature ducks magically in flight inside the box, behind the glass.

Anna was an unparalleled seamstress and an amateur tinkering mechanic, with her piano, her sewing machines, and even her car until she finally stopped driving in the mid-1950s, putting a big humpbacked Ford out to pasture. I heard tell that Anna even tuned up the engine on my grandfather's old launch, that he was mechanically helpless in her presence.

Anna would have enjoyed my boat. I could have brought a scrap of the faded-blue interior material to her, and she would have said:

"Save the old pieces. I can make anything if I have a piece to work with."

7

IN LATE JUNE, one month before the boat was discovered, Emily developed a rash. Jennifer thought it was swimmer's itch, from swimming in White Bear. I was offended that the lake could be charged with such ill treatment of a child, and I defended the home waters, but not vehemently; very soon it was not funny. Emily was getting worse as summer blossomed into the fullness of its long days and short nights. The rash devolved into a fever, the fever into a swelling of her joints. We had her at home under doctor's instructions. She was so listless one Saturday afternoon in July that when Jennifer held her in her arms on a patio swing, lazily moving back and forth, Emily's head moved involuntarily in an unreal way, a little off beat with the rhythm of the swing. She was sickly pale. Her breath was shallow.

Jennifer kept swinging, not saying anything, just crying silently.

"She's burning up," Jennifer said. "Why won't this fever break?"

"It will," I said. "I mean, it has to, doesn't it? Fevers break."

"This isn't right, this just isn't right," Jennifer said. "What if she dies?"

"She won't," I said. I got up, went inside, and called the doctor. When I came back outside I said, "We're putting her in the hospital."

I knew action better than I knew words. I knew how to move better than I knew how to comfort. I didn't know what to do or say to a mother holding a child whom she believed might actually die in her arms. I put myself into movement, walking, dialing the telephone, reaching the doctor, communicating our alarm.

Emily was hospitalized for a week. Jennifer stayed in Emily's room virtually the entire time, sleeping fitfully, if at all, on a hospital cot. The diagnosis was made after everything else, including various cancers, was ruled out. Emily had Still's disease, a form of juvenile arthritis that had such a grip on her that her liver and spleen had become swollen. Even her heart was threatened until her fever broke, which it finally did three days after her hospital admittance. All we could do was touch her, comfort her, talk to her, read to her, promise her that she would be all right, which were words and comforts that Jennifer, Andy, and I used on each other. We didn't know if she would be all right. Jennifer felt Emily's illness. I am sure of that. I am sure that Jennifer felt the delirium of Emily's fever, the aching of her joints, and the sick dryness at the back of Emily's throat, and I know for certain that Jennifer felt the burning of the needle every one of the dozens of times that Emily had blood drawn from her bruised arm.

I am sure that Jennifer would easily have traded places with Emily. I am positive of that. I could only learn from Jennifer, stand back and try to learn that kind of intuitive aliveness for another. Jennifer had been teaching me a great deal about emotional awakenings and commitments in our time together. I advanced and stumbled and advanced and stumbled again. I am not sure what I felt about Emily. I felt as though I didn't have the tools to understand the seriousness of her illness. It was inconceivable to me that she could die. That was the only strength I could offer the child. I absolutely would not, or could not, accept the possibility that she could not beat whatever it was that held her down.

Slowly, as her liver and spleen returned to normal size, her immune system kicked back into action. Slowly she regained the qualities that made her Emily—feistiness, anger, laughter through her gapped baby teeth.

When we got her back home she was weak, thin, and stiff-jointed. The physical Emily, the cartwheeling, dancing, twirling, running, jumping, and tree-climbing Emily, the Emily who hit the deck during sirens and weather warnings, took longer to reappear. She bruised easily, her blood thin from an adult regimen of aspirin. She was afraid, too, afraid of a recurrence, which we were told could happen in six weeks or sixteen years or never.

Into late July and then into August, as she slowly regained her strength, Emily often came out to the garage and sat on a trailer tire, just to talk to me or ask questions or beg to be given an assignment. She sorted a thousand screws that summer, putting the slotted heads into one can and the Phillips heads into another. Her brother retained his enthusiasm, too. Andy, in fact, was the one who first laid out my tools surgeon-style. He also sanded the seat backs and other simple, flat pieces. The two of them helped me to keep the shop clean.

Jennifer was pregnant. She looked different during her pregnancies and this time, the third time, was no exception, although it might have been. But not even the hours of lost sleep during Emily's illness could dull Jennifer's strength or the alertness she had for people, principally her children but also people in general. She was attuned to people and not to the things that people made. Having a boat around made no more sense to Jennifer than having a Civil War cannon mounted on our roof.

"Where is the practicality in such a project?" she seemed to ask with every tentative step she took into the garage, her growing belly going through the door a second before the slim rest of her. "Where is the prudence? Show me the economic plausibility of this dilapidated old thing."

Her initial blunt antagonism had at least softened to a reluctant acceptance. It was Jennifer, after all, who introduced Ray to the project. And if the boat was in fact taking up half the garage, if its presence threatened her with the demands it made on my time, she also knew exactly where to find me. There was a comfort in all of us being around that summer, my first summer at home after ten years on the road as a sportswriter.

I remember standing on a ramp at Shea Stadium once, just about sunset, the Twins and Yankees on the field during the summer of the renovation of Yankee Stadium when the Yankees borrowed the Mets' park. I stood on that ramp looking west at the distant skyscrapers of Manhattan in the red summer dusk, and, further out on the horizon, I looked for home, wondering what I was missing.

Now I was done with Minneapolis, done with sportswriting. I was finally working where I had wanted to work eleven years earlier, when I had first started looking for a newspaper job: in St. Paul, writing a general column for the *St. Paul Pioneer Press Dispatch*.

* * *

The goal in the late summer and autumn of 1984 was to make the show in the summer of 1985. Although I knew this was improbable, it seemed helpful to set an unreasonable goal as protection against my growing weary of something I was spending so much time with. I did something to the boat on a daily basis, some days spending only a matter of minutes, but other days spending hours. The immediate task was the repair of all the side planks. Virtually all of them had been removed to make the task of sistering up the braces easier, or to make room for the stem surgery, or at the very least to refasten the planks. I made the sides tight again with new screws to replace the broken ones I extracted with a needle-nose pliers.

As an example of how the boat had deteriorated over the years, the two bottommost side planks, the ones that were scribed with the waterline, had been painted so often and so clumsily over the years that the waterline not only had been obscured but had been repainted above the original markings. With the waterline marked so imprecisely, the boat, like an unkempt man, had the appearance of wearing its trousers too high over the waist.

I used paint remover and a heat gun to remove as much paint as possible from both those planks, working on them on the garage floor. I had music on, the big door open to the gently approaching autumn. It was not at all a dispiriting job. It was archaeological. Removing layer after layer of old chalky paint took me closer and closer to the real thing, the original thing. The bottom, I discovered, was green, an indescribably beautiful green of the shade seen in the striped porch awnings of our old cottage.

Bud's utility had a copper-bronze-colored bottom. It got shipped from Algonac with a green bottom like the one I was now discovering, but in the days when Johnson's maintained all the boats on the lake, they practiced convenience. If copper bronze was what was available, copper bronze is what was used. To be fair to Johnson's, they usually had in stock what was current, and since most post–World War II Chris Crafts had the copper-colored bottoms, boats maintained by Johnson's naturally enough lost their green- or red-bottomed heritages as these boats survived into the 1950s.

Typically—it is even more common among restored automobiles—the boats displayed at in-water shows in the 1980s are in many respects finer craft than they were ever intended to be. They are so perfect and clean that meals might be eaten off the engine blocks or in the deepest recesses of the bilge. In 1951, to pick a year arbitrarily, my boat was somebody's highly practical and absolutely unspectacular fourteen-year-old boat. Paint it up over the winter. Throw a canvas over it. Break it out again in May. Use it, for fishing, for partying, for waterskiing, for towing sailboats.

Use it.

Johnson's sheds were packed with stored motorboats in the thirties, forties, fifties, and sixties. By 1970, when sailboat construction at Johnson's had become almost exclusively of fiberglass, the wood speedboats on the lake declined porportionately. They began to vanish, just as the wood sailboats had, and were just as rarely discovered. In the summer of 1985, I came across one of Johnson's most elegant scows, a twenty-eight-foot E class, its cedar hull rotting away in the side yard of a house in Mahtomedi, back up off the lake. This E boat was thirty, thirty-five years old. Two or three of its hull planks were missing, exposing ribs that looked trellislike.

Some motorboats were burned. Some were purposely sunk. Some were junked. I now know of clairvoyants who prowled around Johnson's in the summer of 1969 and negotiated dirt cheap prices on rare little pieces that had been sitting in the sheds for years—a 1941 seventeen-foot Chris Craft Deluxe runabout comes to mind. A couple of hundred dollars took that one away. There were fifty-gallon drums full of hardware, too, flag staffs, engine parts. Many of the drums were hauled to the junkyards. In the summer of 1982 I found a pre–World War II Chris Craft stern flagpole, with its distinctive green-tinted glass-globe light, in what possibly was the last barrel of sweepings left in the basement of the boat works—a boat works, incidentally, that had become so haute couture in the 1980s that it had its own line of sports clothing, cocktail glasses, and foul-weather gear.

I was working in the garage one night after supper with the overhead door open to the alley and the service door open to the backyard, which was pretty from my odd, cramped angle on it. I was sitting in the bilge of the boat, looking out through the exposed stern. Evening light played into the shade of the crab apple tree. There was haze in the light, like a sprinkling of gold dust.

Emily snuck up on me. She went right past me in the garage and said, "Hi there, Dad," knowing where I was. I pulled myself up and looked at her over the edge of the boat. There was a spring in her step; she was getting better.

"Hi there, yourself."

I suppose I had become a joke, disappearing into that bilge. As a precaution, I always left the garage doors open as a signal to my family that, my disappearances notwithstanding, I was always available to be hailed. Sometimes one or the other of them would, in fact, hail me, and I would scramble out of the bilge and pretend that I was not at all preoccupied.

Emily stopped in the middle of the alley and pirouet-ted, as though she had reached the center of a stage, only it was just the alley—telephone poles and overhanging wires; dented garbage cans; the narrow, crowned roadway; the sign that said Speed Limit 5, Children Playing.

Emily said, "Turn up the radio."

Her arms were folded across her chest, and her head was tilted a couple of degrees. If there was mischief in her eyes I couldn't see it. She was backlit in the fading daylight so that the dull wash illuminated the ends of her brown hair and shadowed her face around the folds of her hooded sweatshirt. She had had the good sense to insist on a short haircut for summer, before she got sick. She thought it was splendid before she got sick to have short hair, and then she didn't think much about it at all because when she got sick her hair stopped growing. She stopped growing.

"Hey, come on," she said, "turn up the radio. Loud."

"Where's Mom?" I said.

"In the house."

"What's your brother doing?"

"I don't know."

I jumped down, making a cloud of sanding dust. This was the way it was supposed to happen. If she was going to get better, she was going to get better on her own be-cause there wasn't any medicine for what ailed her except time. And aspirin, of all things. For Christ's sake, aspirin. How much aspirin could a six-year-old stomach?

I turned up the paint-splattered workbench radio for her: "Jump," the Van Halen song. She took off dancing in the alley, like a wild girl. It looked like a combination of the Charleston and Jazzercise.

"All right, Emily!"

She didn't even look up. Her arms were flying in one

direction and her legs in another. She was concentrating, biting her pale bottom lip, trying to jump when the band sang, "Jump!"

I backed out of the garage slowly, afraid that she might stop if she saw me leave. I backed all the way from the garage to the house, watching her through the opening in the service door. It was like watching her through the wrong end of a telescope. In a stage whisper I said, "Jennifer, Jennifer." She came to the window of the family room at the back of the house. I said, "Emily's dancing, in the alley. You've got to see this."

Andy came up behind his mother.

"What's the deal?" he said.

"Emily's dancing, in the alley."

Andy raced around inside the house and came out the side door; Jennifer didn't move. "I can see her from here," she said.

"Come out to the garage," I said again, "come out and see your dancing wonder."

Jennifer slid the family room door open and came out that way. Out in the garage Andy was leaning up against the side of the boat.

"Do it, Emily," Andy said.

She was still going strong, adding a smile now to the performance.

"Weeeee, ooooo," she said.

Her arms went skyward, to the right and to the left. She kicked her legs out, too, a small cyclone in the middle of the alley. She danced until she just about keeled over.

"You guys," Emily said, "quit staring."

Jennifer stayed outside in the backyard, walking to one corner of it and back. She draped her arms over a branch of the crab apple tree. Andy took off on his bike.

Emily came back through the garage, exhausted.

"Hi, Dad."

"Hi yourself."

Working on my boat, letting my mind drift and my hands play over the freshly sanded mahogany, it was easy to feel a kinship with the past, to remember Johnson's, for example, the way it was when Bud's utility was stored and maintained there and ultimately turned over to them, as though to authorities who intended to close the book on an era.

The harder I worked on my boat, the further back in time I went, certainly to times before I was born. Even the original waterline scribes were at last visible on my boat, thick creamy white paint visible between the scribed lines. I had to be careful not to sand the lines off. You could see how handsome it would be with that pure white ribbon between the green bottom and mahogany siding. By reclaiming those bottommost side boards, I reclaimed that much more visible mahogany, restoring beauty to boards that had been inaccurately and entirely painted over with copper-bronze paint.

Before refastening those boards, I laid in a trail of adhesive caulk along the rabbit in the chine. When we finally launched the '47 Sportsman the previous summer, it had leaked drastically all along the chine. My boat wouldn't.

Some days I worked only on projects that had little to do with the hull itself. I removed every piece of interior paneling, six pieces to an interior side, and sanded each one to bare, peach-colored mahogany, filling countless tiny nicks and scratches with wine-red wood putty. That kind of work easily accommodated Emily sitting on the workbench, pretending to have a job to do. The interior paneling helped to distinguish the Deluxe from the Standard utility models. The standard model had its ribs and braces exposed. I also removed both the front and rear decks, for two reasons. The deck beams and king plank, fore and aft, were rotted and needed to be replaced. And I also wanted to uniformly clean out the deck seams, so that when I recaulked them they would be perfect. At the shows, it never failed to catch our eyes when a deck was done perfectly. An imperfect deck was visible from fifty yards. I also had all the transom boards off. They were rotted. I had the engine box in the basement, a winter job.

The engine itself, the original Chris Craft flathead six-cylinder Model K, 95-horse, was on blocks in a corner of the garage, a blue, grease-stained thing of beauty, but also a thing of mystery and doubt. We never even removed the engine from the Billy Joe House Sportsman, a 115-horse Chrysler Marine. I had the engine out of the utility first thing, used a tow truck service to hang a boom and hook over the engine and lift it out, nearly 700 pounds worth of serious iron. The tow truck driver and I bet each other the engine had never been out of the boat. The years had made a bond of the metal faces on the collar that coupled the shaft to the transmission in the back of the engine. We used a pry bar and could not break that seal. Only by the driver's slowly lifting the engine while I stayed in the boat and kept pressure on the shaft did the seal finally break, leaving shiny metal on both faces that had been stuck.

If wood was new to me, engines were another world. My automobile maintenance, for example, was limited to changing my own oil and filter. I placed my trust in the mechanics for anything beyond routine lubrication.

I put the boat engine out of mind. I would turn it over to professionals by and by.

* * *

In early August Andy and I went to Cooperstown, New York for Harmon Killebrew's induction into the Baseball Hall of Fame. It was to be a three-day writing weekend, a brief foray back into sportswriting. You would have thought that the world of baseball was as distant from boats as worlds could get, except that the village of Cooperstown, set on the east shore of Lake Otsego, was an eerie throwback to lakeside villages in the 1940s. The lake itself was long and narrow, wandering away from Cooperstown like a river disappearing into the enchanted Appalachian foothills. After checking in at the Cooperstown Motel we walked five or so elm- and oak-shaded blocks into the village, reconnoitering the Hall of Fame itself as well as the Otesaga Hotel, where the inductees were lodged in the opulence of another era, high ceilings and carpet as green and thick as a stack of money. We hung around the ancient lobby long enough for Andy to get autographs, including Killebrew's, and then we strolled over to the town docks. There was something under a cover there, something familiar, the way it gently bobbed and tugged at itself in a slip. It was under full smoke-colored canvas, to the waterline.

"Hey, what hey!" I said.

We walked out to the slip, and I bent down and peeled back the canvas.

"Holy, holy," I said.

"A Chris Craft?" Andy said.

"I'll say, a 1929 or 1930. A rare one."

The humidity was clinging. The lake was still, glassy-looking. The boat's windshield was enormous, some of the chrome worn off to show the brassy metal under it. The steering wheel was wooden. I peeled off more canvas to see the original round bow light, yellowed, striped lines on the front deck. We were alone on the docks. I looked at the boat for ten minutes before I folded the canvas back into place, gently, as though I were covering bones in an archaeological dig.

We ate dinner that evening at a restaurant at the foot of the docks. Through the porthole windows we watched the sun set as it burned orange behind the haze. Afterwards we were walking along a dark and leafy sidewalk back up the hill to our motel when an old Buick with running boards turned the corner and chugged by, its yellowish headlights making twin beams through the thick summer darkness. I put my hand on Andy's head as we walked and let it stay there a moment. There was something wonderful in the air, something I couldn't put my finger on, something about the ring of coincidence in finding an old utility boat and then getting conveniently installed for a few summer days and nights in a village that hadn't changed much since the 1940s.

The next day we thoroughly toured the Hall of Fame, Andy a walking baseball encyclopedia. I took him back to the Otesaga, too, for the official autographing session of the inductees. The old ballplayers were seated under green-and-white funeral tents on the sprawling lawn of the lodge that sloped down to the shore of the lake. Another hot day, the lake still. I kept my eye on Andy from an umbrella table on the flagstone porch overlooking the lawn. When Andy returned at last from his wait in the autograph lines he performed a devastating imitation of one of the ballplayers bringing a cup of coffee to his lips. Andy's hands shook and his lips trembled as he mimicked the ballplayer taking a sip of coffee.

We gravitated back to the docks that afternoon and met the owner of the Chris Craft. He looked to be lawyerish, mid-forties, keeping his conversational distance. He was preparing to go out on a Saturday afternoon ride. We attempted to strike up a conversation as he rolled back his canvas, showing the cockpits cluttered with bumpers and life jackets. He told me how he found the boat in upstate New York and had done nothing to it except refinish it. I told him about my utility back home.

"Don't see many of those," he said. He was joined on the dock by children and neighbors who had been up in the parking lot next to the restaurant with the porthole windows.

"Or these," I said, indicating his boat, now fully uncovered, the smell of it released and then the boat smell mingling with the smell of the summer day.

We stayed put until the owner departed, watching the narrow stern leave its tidy wake until he cleared the docks. He was quite a ways out before he gave it more gas, and then they were racing down the wooded shoreline, making a rooster tail of foam.

On Sunday afternoon, the afternoon of Killebrew's induction, the lake was agleam through the trees, that special kind of sparkling when the sun catches the tips of the waves and jewel-like bursts of light flicker across the surface of the water. The humidity made a summer haze on the grounds of the Hall of Fame, and grown men became damp and mopped their brows. Women fanned themselves with the induction program or stayed under the shade of parasols.

Killebrew, still holding his blocky, 200-pound playing weight, his hands gripping the sides of his lectern, reminisced about how his mother would watch him and his brother playing ball in the front yard of their house in Payette, Idaho, and then complain to their father that the boys were ruining the grass.

"We're not raising grass here, Mother," Harmon quoted his late father to the silent crowd in Cooperstown, "we're raising boys."

Even the loud, cantankerous fans—who had come from Brooklyn to remind the high priests of baseball that the Dodgers should never have been allowed to leave—fell silent as Killebrew's voice grew thick with the memories of his dead father.

I looked up at Harmon on the speaker's platform, sweat glistening on his handsome bald head, and then I looked out at Lake Otsego, winking in bursts and sparkles. The summers of Killebrew's prime were precisely the summers of my boyhood prime, on the water at White Bear when I was Andy's age, so that I felt some deep connection to Harmon and to water, to Andy, to Bud, to the way summers are linked so inexhaustibly by days at the lake and at the ballpark. For me, the ballpark was a remote place, a city place, and I was connected to it only by the radio. In 1961, Harmon's first year in Minnesota, he hit forty-six home runs, the first of three straight prime-time years for the both of us. In 1961 I soloed in the utility. In 1962 Harmon hit forty-eight home runs. I won a sailing championship, Bud always following the races, cruising slowly alongside the race course, the last summer he would own the utility. In 1963 (Harmon: forty-five round-trippers) we were using the Boat that Broke Loose from the Car, a bigger, slightly more modern boat.

Our last night in Cooperstown, Andy and I saw *The Natural* at the Otsego on Main Street, the movie's booking timed to coincide with the Hall of Fame inductions, especially ironic considering that Killebrew came as close as any ballplayer I could think of to matching Bernard Malamud's Roy Hobbs. In fact Killebrew, who had impressed scouts by smashing home runs deep into potato fields back home, traveled by train, rubelike, to his major league debut with the Senators in 1954. After the show, Andy and I walked up and down Main Street, crowded with tourists like us, in town for the induction. I was going to tell Andy that in the book, Hobbs took the bribe, he didn't hit the home run. But then I saw the glory of the movie home run in Andy's eyes, and I thought better than to blow the whistle.

When we walked back up the hill to our motel, the moon made a pale, ghostly light in the wooded hills around the village, and the only sound was the song of crickets. Around 1 A.M. the village siren went off. What a terrible start it was. It didn't have the metallic urgency or tempo of a city siren. It was an old-fashioned, deep-throated howl of a warning.

There was a clamoring of feet hitting the floorboards in the Cooperstown Motel, whose guests, throwing on robes, stepped out into the blackness. Andy and I went to the window and drew back the curtain.

"I'm going outside," I said.

"Is it a fire?" he said.

"Probably."

"Not here, though?"

"No, not here. Good thing Emily isn't with us."

"She'd be under the bed," Andy said, trying to be brave himself.

Out on the deck the siren was so piercing that you had to plug your ears. Everyone kept waiting for the reassuring sound of fire trucks going through their gears; the fire hall was just three blocks down the road. But nobody ever did hear the trucks.

"What is it?" strangers were asking each other outside.

"A fire?"

"A storm, maybe."

"Too cool for a storm."

I remembered a night from long ago, in Mahtomedi, when I was Andy's age or a little younger, when an old mansion back off the lake burned in a spectacular fire that reached at the sky on a still, humid summer night. That house was nearly a mile from ours, but the fire made a halo of light in the distance, red and sparking and frightening. We knew the house and we knew it to be old and foreboding, surrounded by a stone fence with a creaky wood gate between stone pillars in the front. Either I really remember it or I imagined that motorboats nosed up to the edge of the pool of light that the fire cast on the lake near the shore, the bow lights of the boats making a semicircle of red and green, red and green, and red and green, at the edge of the eerie light on the water. The next morning there was a falling of ash in our yard, delicate scrolls of ash that disintegrated to the touch.

This night in Cooperstown had the same strange feel of foreboding, of stillness, as though we somehow had spun back in time. I stole my anxious glances at the crest of the hills, illuminated in that Sleepy Hollow light of the pale moon.

And then the siren quit, dying out in a moan. The crickets started singing again.

"Go back to bed," I told Andy.

Perhaps an hour passed. Andy had long since fallen asleep, his sweet breath sighing out of his slightly open mouth. I was just falling to sleep myself when the siren went off again.

"Hey, what, Dad, hey?" Andy said, pushing up out of bed with his eyes still closed.

"It's OK," I said.

I went to the window and didn't see a thing. The

other guests were assembling again outside, and I joined them.

"Maybe it's a prank," somebody said.

"Has to be a fire."

"There," somebody said, pointing. "There's a police car."

The blue strobe lights of a police car could be seen through the haze, coming our way fast and then speeding past, going south toward Milford or Hartwick or Hyde Park. It was a relief. Another silent response to the siren would have left too much to the imagination. The siren quit for a second time, and the rest of the night was silent, although we kept thinking we heard the trailing moan of the siren.

The morning was fresh and blue. We drove by the town docks on the way out of town. A corner of the canvas had blown off the old Chris Craft. Sunshine caught a chrome corner of the square windshield and made a brief blinding starburst of light before I turned my head away.

8

THE BOAT WAS PUT UP FOR THE WINTER two garages down
the alley east of our house, in the second stall of the garage
belonging to a woman who recently had been widowed. I
shoveled her sidewalk and garage apron on the alley in exchange for the storage. On sunny winter days, with the
temperature climbing into the thirties, she washed her new
Chevrolet Cavalier in the sun-drenched alley, always to the
accompaniment of a radio station that played 1940s swing
music, the old big band mood music that always put me in
mind of intimate nightclub tables, with white linens and
fringed lampshades on the table lights. I'd walk in on the
boat, or I'd get into it if I had to fetch her snow rake down
from the rafters, and I could hear her as she hummed along
to the bluesy ballads.

There is an elemental satisfaction in sheltering body
and soul and boats from the weather. It was reassuring to
enter the garage after a big snow and study the boat in the
cold stillness, to have put it away clean and dry for the first
time in ten, twenty, thirty years. Who knew? Menth sug-

gested that the man he bought it from appeared to be in a hurry, possibly a man on the move, a man who had no knowledge of the boat's history or was disinclined to share the history he did have.

One of the first things I did when I got the boat was send the serial number, 17144, along with twenty-five dollars, to what was left of Chris Craft's ancestral home at Algonac, Michigan. In return, I was sent a copy of the boat's original shipping invoice informing me that my boat was, in fact, built in Algonac, not in one of the satellite plants, and was shipped out on November 1, 1937, carrying a list price of $1,240.

I went there once, to Algonac, making a pilgrimage. During Super Bowl week in Detroit, in January of 1982, I got up early one midweek morning, signed out a National Football League courtesy car and drove out to Algonac. I didn't bother to ask anyone to go with me. No one would have understood; it seems axiomatic that sportswriters, especially the ones at the national level, are city born and bred and have no more interest in old boats than they do in rocketry or quilting.

The NFL had us quartered out in Dearborn. I drove east on I-75, past the Ford World Headquarters, then past Ford's Rouge Plant where, as a Detroit cab driver once told me, "You got a pile a dirt and iron pellets at one end of the plant and out the other end comes a automobile."

Detroit, bathed in an icy mist, looked menacing and stark in the cold vapors rising off the Detroit River, the black glass towers of the riverfront Renaissance Center looking like industrial smokestacks. The countryside changed and grew more recognizable in the suburbs north of the big city, through St. Clair Shores, Roseville, Mt. Clemens. Just before New Baltimore, I got off the interstate and went east on Michigan 29, a narrow ribbon of low two-lane highway through Achorville, New Haven, Pearl Beach, and at last into Algonac, where the St. Clair River empties into Lake St. Clair, where Edsel Ford and Gar Wood and Christopher Columbus Smith and a generation of their like-minded pals did their speedboat racing.

With the exception of the extraordinary estates on Lake St. Clair, I might as well have been driving out White Bear way at home, the country was so familiar, the promise of water so near.

It was on the St. Clair River and Lake St. Clair that Chris Craft executives, wearing white shirts and ties, posed in their boats for publicity and advertising photographs. Taking publicity shots at this spot always intrigued me: instead of a leafy shoreline in the background, which Madison Avenue might have insisted on, there were distant smokestacks and shorefront warehouses, a hint of industrialization, a vaguely cold and urban scene—and yet the promise of escape behind the wheel of the pictured runabout.

Now I knew why. Although at the turn of the century it was a considerably distant summer colony, by the 1930s and 1940s Algonac had become virtually a suburb of Detroit, with its long industrial reach along the interconnecting waterways made by the Detroit River, Lake St. Clair, and the St. Clair River. Chris Craft photographs were often taken with Detroit quite literally in the background. And because new models always came off the assembly line in the fall, when Chris Craft's seasonal workers were furloughed, it looked cold because it quite probably was.

Algonac came into being as Point du Chene in 1800, and then it was known successively as Plainfield, Clay, Manchester, and finally, in 1843, Algonac, from "the land of the Algonquin."

Christopher Columbus Smith, native born to Algonac, was once its postmaster, member of its school board, and, curiously enough, the proprietor of its first telephone exchange. He hunted in the St. Clair flats in a home-built rowing skiff so vastly superior to those of his fellow townfolk that they commissioned him to build the skiff for public sale. In 1884 Chris and his oldest son, Jay, experimented with a naphtha-gasoline engine in one of Chris's long rowing launches, and thus was created the crude inboard that was to become the foundation of the family's fortune.

I used the Detroit Public Library when I covered baseball at Tiger Stadium. There is such surprisingly little material on Chris Craft there that I began to believe that either Smith—who died in 1939, one of his obituary photographs showing a comically round-faced man wearing what looked to be a porkpie hat because of the way the brim was folded up a turn all the way around—was eccentrically private or news reporters were so overwhelmed by the magnificence of automobile and steel production that an upriver family boat builder was easily overlooked, even as he was becoming the world's largest standardized builder of pleasure craft.

By 1906, Smith had hooked up with a boat-racing promoter named John J. Ryan, to form the Smith-Ryan boat company, principally to make step-bottomed racing hulls, including a twenty-six-footer that went eighteen miles per hour. Ryan quit in 1913, and Smith enlisted his sons, Jay, Bernard, Owen, and Hamilton, and daughter, Catherine, to run the firm as a family business.

Smith struck it rich in 1914. That was the year he built the famous *Miss Detroit* for Garfield Arthur Wood, the son of a Lake Osakis, Minnesota, ferryboat operator. Gar Wood, who had become wealthy by inventing a hydraulic lift that removed coal from trucks, bought Smith's boatyard in Algonac and commissioned him to build the gentleman racers for which Gar Wood became famous. Ultimately, Wood and Smith parted amicably so that Wood, too, might build his own line of speedboats and runabouts.

Miss Detroit turned 48.5 miles per hour. In 1916, Jay and Bernard drove *Miss Minneapolis* to 66.66 miles per hour. It was specifically as a result of the success of his racing boats that by 1920, Smith and his family—once again without partners—had exclusively begun to build runabouts. The demand for pleasure craft was created most specifically by the publicity generated by racing.

In the 1930s Chris Craft employed upwards of 650 men at Algonac and hundreds of others at satellite plants. Algonac had a town foundry. Chris Craft had its own engine works, machine shops, rail spurs, and water tower. Chris Craft was its own place. In 1982 I discovered a modern brick-faced storefront building. The outbuildings, vast sheds with hangarlike roofs, were vacant. Scrub weeds stuck up through the dirty snow.

Windows were broken. The rail spurs had been grown over with brush; the land was soon to be developed into a private condominium and marina complex. A fellow named Joe Morrison was inside the Chris Craft store. The last man, he seemed to be. He sold a few conveniently stocked supplies and retrieved on microfilm the requests for shipping invoices that he received from people like me.

Morrison and I made small talk. I told him about my Sportsman and my search for a utility, and while not an unfriendly man, he evidently had developed a skin of disinterest, possibly as a protection against any hope at all of the old way of life coming back.

Chris Craft's corporate and manufacturing headquarters had been located in Florida since the early 1960s. Now there was just Morrison and a woman working in an office. She had red hair, piled atop her head in a cotton candy swirl. The showroom was dimly lit, dull wood paneling on the walls, metal shelves. I felt obligated to buy something and left there with a set of Chris Craft decals for the Billy Joe House twenty-two-footer.

All the way back to Detroit I listened to a call-in show; the natives were angry at the way they perceived *Sports Illustrated* to be taking Detroit apart as an inhospitable host to the Super Bowl. There exists on the face of the earth no more spoiled breed of laborer than the common sportswriter, including myself, who cannot tolerate the idea of spending expense account money in Detroit in January. I should have had some of my pals along to see Algonac, especially in the melancholy light of a late winter's afternoon.

I suspect that most people who restore old boats like to know where they have been, a human history to bring life to the wood. When Menth acquired his utility from the original owner in northern Minnesota, he also acquired early photographs of the boat, sales information, a bill of sale, a handwritten diary of the owner's use of it, all the material conspiring to make Menth believe that he had acquired not so much a workable Chris Craft, but an heirloom.

One of the reasons I wanted to find my father's old utility was the obvious notion that I knew its history. Besides, theoretically it could still exist. My grandfather's boat, to take the connection to water a generation deeper, could not possibly still exist, and yet by knowing about it I felt a certain kinship that marked my place in a long line of motorboat operators, back to the days when such a claim involved a degree of risk and adventure. At the same time that Smith and Gar Wood were creating a demand for pleasure craft by racing their sleek, stripped-down hulls, Henry Soucheray, my grandfather, was racing a launch he kept at White Bear, in a slip of water he dredged out of the shoreline in front of his cottage, and where, to this day, traces of the stone footings that defined the slip are still visible.

My father, as off-handedly as if he were offering me a match or a stick of gum, one day slid an envelope across the front seat of his car and said, "I thought you might enjoy these." My hounding him for information had begun to pay dividends in the later years of his life. He was occasionally leaking me documents, sometimes as casually as a horseplayer giving a tip.

Inside this latest envelope were a dozen pictures of his mother and father at the cottage at White Bear Lake. They dated to before my father's birth. More remarkably, one of the pictures was of my grandfather's launch, with its high-crowned canvas deck. I had only heard about this boat; I had never seen it. My grandfather was sitting at the wheel. His wife, my grandmother Anna, was seated in the back in a wicker chair, looking small under a stern pole and a stern flag that looked as big as a bed sheet. I could not believe the pictures. One of them showed a motorboat race, a big brown launch racing what I presumed to be my grandfather's white one. There was a name on my grandfather's boat, on the starboard bow, the name apparently underscored by an arrow. I could make out the arrow, but to my dismay, the name above it was indecipherable.

Two of the photographs clearly showed the lagoon that had been dug out of the shoreline, a pile of fresh sand at the entrance to the lagoon and a footbridge constructed of loose timbers and planks across the water of the lagoon. The shoreline somehow looked primitive, the cottages prominent with screens and awnings. Other shots showed my grandparents swimming, posed for the camera with their backs to the dock. They wore bathing suits that covered nearly their entire bodies.

The picture of the boat, the launch, was fantastic. I never knew either of my grandfathers, and yet here was one of them posed in a way that was so entirely familiar that I felt slightly spooked.

"When was this?" I asked my father.

"Nineteen ten, nineteen twelve, before me," he said.

It was the way the man, my grandfather, sat at the wheel, like my father sat at the wheel, as I anticipated I would sit at the wheel. He wore a white shirt, buttoned at the neck, khaki trousers, a belt. He had a canvas cap on, like a motorman's cap, with a dark shiny visor. His right hand was on the starboard gunnel, the fingers delicately holding the trim piece around the gunnel in such a way that reminded me of my own hands; I am self-conscious about my hands, believing them to be too thin. His left hand was on the back of the vacant wicker chair next to his. There was wind, from the west, the stern of the boat swung to shore. Henry had his jaw dropped a degree or so to keep the wind from getting under the visor of the cap. He was looking into the camera.

My grandmother was behind him, smiling broadly. She wore a big-brimmed straw hat, her right hand clamped down on the top if it to keep it from blowing off. The wind had blown the rim of the hat back, Poncho Villa style, and she seemed to be laughing at the task of holding onto the hat.

That picture, maybe eighty years old, figured into the scheme of my own project. Also in the boat was one of my grandmother's sisters, Mame, her coal-black hair severely parted in the middle, a streak of scalp showing between the fields of black hair. She was Jack Donohue's mother—Jack

Donohue, my father's cousin and one of his best friends. Jack Donohue owned my father's utility before my father did.

It was there in the picture, what I sometimes feel when I am standing on the dock or standing on the shore at White Bear: the feeling of activity, the murmuring of the voices that started it all, the life on the water getting passed down from hand to hand, generation to generation.

I wanted to find the boat, Bud's utility, that family hands had touched virtually from the day it was new. And family hands had marked it, as though with clues in the event it was ever searched for. There were seven clues in all, all of which I discovered by studying 1950s Polaroid snapshots in family photo albums, snapshots that come up the line, generationally, to include not grandparents but my own brothers and sisters posed in the utility tied to the dock in the same waters as the old launch.

One, the utility had a water temperature gauge. Chris Craft did not install such gauges. Johnson's must have put it in, probably sometime in the 1950s.

Two, it had a distinctive chrome post on the front deck, between the bow light and the lifting ring, a fat little chrome stub with a T on it, a bollard.

Three, it had a white steering wheel. That wheel was almost certainly black when the boat was new.

Four, it had a hand-operated spotlight mounted just where the driver's hand would rest when the driver placed his right arm in repose on the covering board.

Five, the spotlight switch hung vertically from the dash, next to the steering column.

Six, the interior paneling had been painted an olive-drab color. My father once told me that the workmen at Johnson's, presumably with the blessing of the pragmatic Iver Johnson (the boss of the brothers Johnson), used brown paint for filler stain when they refinished powerboats.

Seven, a chrome Chris Craft emblem was screwed into the dash. The emblem was in the post World War II–style Chris Craft script.

People touring state fairs and claiming to display Al Capone's car, could, I suppose, fool me. But if I ever saw Bud's utility I would know it as his. The clues were strong and telling. I let Menth onto them once. His boat, his company, became an annual attraction at the boat shows I was desperate to enter. He was such a kindred spirit and so impossibly enthusiastic that my cynical nature at first refused to believe that such a man could exist.

Menth, too, had grown up on a lake—Minnetonka. He, too, remembered the boats from his youth. He somehow understood that I intended to attach mystical significance to the task if I ever found a utility of my own.

For the first thirty-five years of my life, which paralleled the best thirty-five years of life for men of my father's generation, my father's health and vitality was so unquestionably consistent that a breakdown in his health was inconceivable. I don't believe he ever suffered a cold. I know for a fact that he was never tardy or absent, from either work or social engagement. He once made of a broken ankle an act of dry comedy. He broke the ankle in the late 1960s, snow skiing. Lying on the hill, intrigued by his floppy ankle, he said, "I'll be damned."

When the ski patrol came, put him on a litter, and took him off the hill, he half-rose up on the cot and put his right hand to left shoulder and his left hand to right shoulder, creating the image of a pharaoh getting a lift through ancient streets.

Beginning with a heart attack he suffered on my

birthday, January 7, 1978, while playing squash, his health began a slow decline that motivated me in my own way, with the boats, to think about him and his life, our time on the water.

Most specifically, I wondered why our communications, however unintentionally, avoided the emotional dimensions of life. I don't at all mean to suggest that we didn't understand each other or that our relationship lacked depth. Rather, the opposite was true. I am weary of my contemporaries who pretend no identification or communication with their own fathers. You must, as Jennifer insists, take what you are given. My father and I understood each other deeply. It was how that intrigued me. On each occasion of his hospital stays, for example, as I would attempt to get close to him, to clumsily comfort him, he remained characteristically formal, loosening a little when we talked about boats. We must have appeared comically inept at dealing with one another. His infirmities embarrassed him; they prolonged an awkward silence between us. Once he was in the hospital with excruciating pain that just soon enough was diagnosed as an abdominal aneurysm. His back was killing him, almost literally. For him to admit as much was astonishing.

"My back is killing me," he said. He sat on the edge of the bed, his freckled back exposed behind the open flap of the hospital pajamas.

I sat down beside him and rubbed his back, hesitant to touch his back at first and then thinking, to hell with my own hesitancy.

He cleared his throat, like a professor, and said, "You don't have to do that."

"I know I don't have to," I said. "I'd hope that if I was in the hospital and my back was killing me that you'd rub it. Jesus H. Christ."

He allowed me to rub it, although I don't think it had any effect on the pain.

"Thank you," he said, as though I had just handed him change at the hardware store.

And then we began talking about boats.

I laughed, behind him, out of the lines of his peripheral vision.

Boats were our emotion. That was it in a nutshell. I knew instinctively that boats were the medium of a complex relationship full of trapdoors, beneath which were treasures of admiration and respect and love, all of it hidden from free and easy dispensation to each other. I once got a sailboat for Christmas. He had his secretary create a document after the fashion of a gift certificate. When I opened it, it read, "This spring you are entitled to one new X-boat from Johnson Boat Works."

The X-boat, incidentally, was to replace the X-boat in hand, an old tub that leaked, a boat built by the White Bear rival to Johnson, the Amundson Boat Works. I received that boat one morning when I came down to breakfast. I sat on the side of the counter facing him. He sat facing the lake.

"I bought a boat," he said, taking a sip of coffee from a blue cup that had a network of cracks in it, like veins.

My eyes widened. Before I could say anything he told me about it.

We rarely, if ever, played catch, but we often went sailing when I was very young. He taught me to sail. Sometimes we sailed late enough that we sailed by moonlight, the shoreline a dark line and the tops of the trees a jagged line against the moonlit night. I became so proficient at sailing, so embracing of the modern school of it, that I ended up teaching him a thing or two.

We never hunted, but we fished because fishing put

us in a boat. We never had heart-to-hearts, except once, when I was older and needed counseling about life, I made an attempt to have that inevitable talk that I think sons have with fathers, when finally they screw up the courage to ask their fathers how it is done. Life. Job. Marriage. What's the key, the secret, give me a tip. I swear to God he quite naturally enough steered the conversation into his account of having met a man who knew of a 1962 twenty-three-foot Chris Craft Holiday for sale. My father's solution to emotional crisis, his or his children's, was simple. He bought boats. Together we bought that latest discovery of his. It was a Holiday that I went and found during a howling wind and snow in the winter of 1980.

Winter is too kind a word. Winter suggests that the weather might have been tolerable. It was a January day when I saw that boat, cold and blustery with drifting snow. I drove from St. Paul to the western fringe of Minneapolis—Minnetonka, again and forever, Minnetonka—to get a look at it. I made deep tracks through the falling snow, struggling from the owner's driveway to the side yard where the boat was sitting on a trailer under a windbreak of blue spruce. The trailer was drifted over. The dark-green tarp covering the boat was visible where the snow had blown off. I was able to lift the canvas off for a peek, enough to determine that I wanted the boat. I also got my whiff, worth driving through a storm for. It was an accommodating whiff. It took me back just five months or so, to the previous warm August. I could bottle that perfume here in cabin-fever country and make a fortune.

It wasn't until the spring that I could claim the big boat and truly understand what I had acquired—by getting into the bilge. The bilge produced four screwdrivers, a vice grip, and a roll of electrical tape, an ominous collection of paraphernalia that suggested trouble afloat. I found a tube of Coppertone, too, mid-1960s vintage, so that I imagined a woman in a rather modest bikini by today's standards applying the lotion at sea while her man, dressed in a loud Hawaiian shirt, and probably wearing shorts, and sandals, tried to make repairs as they went adrift.

In the decade after my father's heart attack, as he fought off setback after setback—gallbladder surgery, cataracts, worsening arthritis—it was always the same with him and me. Hard to get through to him, except for that enduring and sacred reference point of things that float. If he was displeased with the antiseptic smells of the hospital, the cheap gowns, the artificial light, the boredom of sitting pitched forward in a chair with his forearms on his knees, he never complained. Actually he complained just once, during a Memorial Day weekend hospital stay to stabilize his erratically beating heart and coincidentally to adjust his heart medication. On that weekend, he thought he was going to die.

"You mean, the way I might say that if I had the flu?" I said. As with Emily, death was inconceivable to me. I hadn't the tools to understand it. I was certain of his hyperbole.

"No," he said. "I mean literally. I think I am going to die."

Because everything had started to go on him, the eyes, the heart. He had suffered a minor stroke, too, and required carotid artery surgery on both sides of his neck over the winter. By Memorial Day weekend he was exhausted, overmedicated, full of despair. He thought he was going to die.

"Your emotions get all screwed up," he told me in the hospital that weekend. I am reasonably certain that it was the first time he ever even used the word *emotion* in my presence.

He started to laugh at the presumed folly of a man's emotions getting screwed up.

And then he started to cry.

9 〜〜〜〜〜〜〜〜〜〜〜〜

MENTH CALLED IN EARLY MARCH, March 1985 now, a hint of spring in the air and a new baby in the house—Stephanie, sleeping in a basket in the window to catch the sun. A month earlier, Jennifer and I had sped to the hospital in the middle of the night, tearing through red lights, hoping like crazy that the cops would give chase so I could shout through my rolled-down window, "Pregnant woman aboard!" and then catch an escort with sirens. No such luck. We didn't see a police car the entire way. We raced through the abandoned streets, mist swirling like smoke around the bulbs in the streetlights.

"I found your dad's boat," Menth said.

It took my breath. He said it conspiratorially, as though he might have looked around the corners in his bank office before speaking into the telephone.

I was on a portable phone, standing above the baby, looking out into the backyard, the sun making slants of light through the crab apple tree. Despite the signs of spring there was still snow in the yard, drifted clumps from an early March blizzard. Melting snow flooded the narrow sidewalk between the house and the garage. I didn't say anything into the telephone. I didn't know what to say; even though Menth always believed that Bud's boat was out there, I never imagined him actually looking for it.

"Impossible," I forced myself to say. I was jealous of Menth, of what he must have felt like at that first moment of discovery.

The odds were astronomically against that boat surviving. Besides, I had done some checking. I had called Buster Johnson three or four times over the years and tried to get him to remember what had become of that boat. Buster confused it with a twenty-two-foot Sportsman that belonged to a friend of my father's.

"No, no," I said, "a little seventeen-footer, with a Model B sixty-horse engine. Flat, folding windshield. Come on, Buster, you remember. It was identical to the starter's boat."

For at least thirty years, probably more, Gene Markoe started all sailboat races at White Bear Lake by firing a cannon bolted to the front deck of the White Bear Yacht Club's own Chris Craft utility. Markoe's boat at anchor—its hull was painted white, but in all other respects it was identical to my father's utility and at least one other utility of the same era on the lake—made one end of the starting line, a buoy the other. I sailed across Gene Markoe's stern a thousand times, waiting for him to pull the string to fire that cannon. Markoe was an ancient man when I was a boy, his pinched, hawklike face bent into the wind, a signpost of my boyhood summers.

"Ah," Buster said, "I can't remember."

Then again, I have never claimed to be the scavenger, the bounty hunter that Menth is. Aside from making a few calls to try and get Buster's brain loosened up, I never conducted a search for that boat. I never beat the bushes, rented a floatplane, rode a snowmobile, swam under a boathouse, breathed my hot breath on secret frosted windows in the winter woods. The only lead I had was the slim one of knowing that the boat was disposed of at the end of the summer of 1962 and that it presumably would not have gone far because by 1962 the boat was considered out of style and certainly not very much in demand. I suspected that somewhere at the boat works were records that would have told what Johnson's did with the boat. I was reasonably certain that Johnson's brokered it; as out of favor as that boat might have been, 1962 was still a good five or six years shy of the era of dumping, burning, and smashing the old ones to kindling.

"I was on business up near Princeton," Menth said, mentioning a small town fifty miles north of the Twin Cities. "A friend of mine named Dick Juul said that if I ever got up near Princeton I should look at a boat he recently bought but hadn't hauled to his own place yet. So I was up near Princeton and decided to take a look. I saw it from a distance, in the backyard of a farm place, trees growing up all around it, and the more I looked, I just had a feeling. And the closer I got to it the stronger the feeling, because the first thing I noticed was where the spotlight was."

"No."

"Little chrome hitching post on the deck, too."

"Come on! White steering wheel?"

"White steering wheel."

"Vertical spotlight switch?"

"It had that. It had a water temperature gauge. I rememberd the snapshots you showed me one time. Dick Juul bought your father's old boat."

I looked down at the sleeping baby and then back out the window, the sun blinding on the snow.

"I have to have it," I said. Menth knew that, of course. There was no other reason for the call. For him, the boat was another quick turnaround.

"I'll have to do some horse trading," Menth said. "They've got it back home in Alexandria now."

"You'll just have to explain to this Juul," I said. "You'll have to tell him that there are circumstances here. This is unbelievable. Trees growing around it?"

"It's in very rough shape."

"I wonder if it's been sitting there since 1962."

"It looks like it could have been."

We talked for a few minutes more, Menth taken up in the improbability of such a curious discovery and his uncanny role in it.

I got out the snapshots that night. In a family that went through as much film as we did, only four black-and-white snapshots of the utility in the summers of 1958 and 1959 managed to get passed down, four black-and-white Polaroids that I had been hoarding. One of them showed my brother Johnny standing in the front seat but facing the stern of the boat for the photographer, presumably my father. Johnny was seven, eight years old, built of baby fat, wearing a T-shirt and madras shorts, pudgy belly showing between shirt and shorts. His right hand was on the top of the windshield. The boat was in the slip under the hoist. The hoist timbers were visible, as well as the dock, the yard, and the concrete wall that was once a breakwater and was only recently knocked down to make room for a more conventional front lawn. In another shot, Johnny and my sister Judy are seated in the front seat, both of them wearing puffy, vest-style life jackets. That shot clearly showed the boat's idiosyncrasies. There was a camp stool in the boat, too, and a coil of rope and a life jacket on the linoleum floor.

The other two shots were long shots. One of them was taken from the shadows of the front yard and looking out at the lake. The boat was tied to the dock and swinging away from it on a south wind. The yard, not yet sodded, was dappled with shade. On a clump of land under a sentry oak on the left side of the yard were the silhouetted backs of my three sisters. There was a playpen in the shade of the yard and two steel lawn chairs, with petal-shaped backs on them as big around as bass drums. The other shot was taken from deeper in the yard, a broad long-distance shot that showed the boat hanging on its hooks.

That boat was special, so intertwined in the memories of my youth, so inescapably a part of me, a part of those endless summer days that were as precious as pearls on a string. It was hard for me to believe that Menth could have stumbled across it; there was something otherworldly about it.

That boat once almost killed me.

Bud was laying patio stones in the front of the house when he noticed that the wind had switched. He suggested that I go down to the dock and pull the boat around and put it up on the hoist. I went. It was a struggle to move the boat around the dock and maneuver it into its slip under the hoist beams. I attached the hoist hooks to the front and rear lifting rings, jumped back to the dock, and then inserted the big black crank handle into a winch with teeth like a picket fence.

I was nine, the first summer of living year-round at the lake. I don't remember how it happened or that I could have prevented it from happening. The boat was out of the water and hanging freely; I had paused, winded from the effort of cranking it up, when the crank handle snapped in half. The winch spun wildly in reverse. The whoosh of the boat dropping back to water made a percussive noise, like a gunshot. In the instant before getting struck, I smelled the hot metal, the friction of the broken cast-iron handle, as shiny where it broke as a vein of silver. One of the broken crank pieces glanced off my left temple and knocked me flying out into the lake, as though shot from a cannon, my arms and legs trailing my body. The numbness in my head was dreamlike. Bud heard either my quick involuntary cry or the loud collapse of the boat. He was then forty-one and suffering the first prolonged attack of the arthritis that would eventually cripple him. He came running. I saw him as though through a kaleidoscope, running through the front yard, a look of agony on his face, his footfalls making explosions of dust on the newly excavated yard, the dust settling back to the ground in slow motion. He appeared to be running in slow motion himself as he ran through the water, taking high marching steps like a drum major to grab the back of my T-shirt and lift me out of the lake.

He ran with me through the yard to the car. I don't remember the trip to the doctor's office. I remember it being later that night and I was at home, my head wrapped in bandages, a welt the size of an egg on the left side of my head, which throbbed with every heartbeat. The television was on—"Perry Mason," then "Oh, Susanna," then "Death Valley Days," then the 10 o'clock news, the one-minute weather, and the sports scores. I was the patient, regarded cautiously, given clear liquids to drink.

We used that winch for another three summers—with a welded handle and a wrap of black electrical tape over the weld joint—before we got rid of it, but I never did crank up that boat again without expecting catastrophe, and to this day I cringe in the presence of cranks, winches, block and tackles, pulleys, and wheels.

*　　*　　*

On the last Saturday in March, me, Bud, Paul, Andy, and one of my brothers-in-law, Mike—a boat show band of us—went to Menth's house. It was a cold, miserable day, wet with a cover of low clouds. We saw the boat from a block away, a dark, water-stained hulk, on a trailer in the driveway, bow pointing toward the street. Menth was waiting for us, pulling a jacket around his shoulders as he came out of the house. Bud was pulled along in the riptide of our excitement; he didn't lead it. I was clamoring around inside the boat, tapping the stem with a hammer, by the time he made it from the car to the boat.

"The stem is solid," I said, in the manner of a man who has learned the hard way to check such things.

It was undeniably the boat in the old snapshots, the boat of the curious white wheel, the afterthought temperature gauge, the oddly placed spotlight switch, the chrome Chris Craft logo in a modern, 1950s script. It was undeniably his boat, or what was left of it in the home stretch of the twentieth century. There were no seat frames, no floor, no gas tank. The front deck had a fist-size hole in it.

But it was the boat. The one we drove out to check on in those long-ago autumns. The boat that snapped the hoist crank. The boat of a thousand excursions and adventures and burbly musical notes of forgotten summers—serial number 17098, the backbone of us—me and him.

Bud didn't say anything. He is not given to fits of excitement. He is not given to bouts of sentiment. I, on the other hand, couldn't stop touching things, the windshield in particular, the wheel, the throttle lever, the shifter, and the wood.

In a subsequent letter accompanying a half-dozen photographs of the boat as he had found it, Juul said he bought the boat from a man named Gil Godderz who had once intended to use the boat at a resort north of Brainerd, in northern Minnesota. For reasons not made entirely clear to Juul—I cannot find Gil Godderz, either—Godderz never put the boat to any resort use. Godderz stored the boat with his niece, on her farm near Princeton, Minnesota. A Godderz nephew, evidently annoyed by the presence of the boat indoors, moved it outside and covered it with a tarp. The tarp rotted off and the boat sat exposed for at least thirteen years, for, as Juul understood it, the boat was discovered and then banished by the nephew in 1972. It is probable that the boat was used from 1962 through 1971, although where remains a mystery and probably will forever.

It took Juul and his son, Tom, a full day to pry the boat and trailer from the ice and frozen clumps of dirt at the Princeton farm. They winched the boat onto a flatbed truck and took it back to Juul's place in the lake country near Alexandria, Minnesota, with every belief that Tom Juul, just then apprenticing as a shipwright, would make the boat his first restoration. When the Juuls got home and began making their own fascinating archaeological discoveries, they made one of the rarest of all. Encased in ice in the bilge under the rear deck was the mahogany stern pole and its decorative pre-war glass globe. The Juuls delicately unearthed it and took it inside to let the ice slowly melt from around the fossilized pole.

My father (as I wrote back to Juul) went through three or four poles a summer, as a result of his absentminded habit of throwing the boat into reverse and backing out of the slip under the hoist timbers in waves that humped the stern high enough out of the water to snap the pole off on either a cross-timber or the dangling heavy hook and pulley.

I cannot possibly imagine what cajoling it might have taken for Menth to pry the boat loose from a father and son obviously as fascinated as I anticipated myself and my father becoming. I suspect that Menth conveyed my urgency and that the Juuls, being fine, feeling fellows, came to understand that the only father and son who might appreciate the boat more than they did were the father and son who once actually owned it. It was a powerful concept; in all my years of attending boat shows I cannot recall having seen a boat shown by the son of the father who once owned it.

"Is it as good as your other one?" Bud said. He was standing stoically in the rain, in Menth's driveway, looking as weathered in his own way as his newly discovered boat.

"Maybe better," I said. "All the bracing seems solid. The hardware is all here." I knew I was falling prey to my own excitement and judging things prematurely, but I didn't care. I was looking at the genuine article.

"I had to give Juul nine hundred dollars for it," Menth said.

"Can I take it home on your trailer?"

"Keep it as long as you need it."

I said I'd be back next weekend with Jennifer's car. On the way back to St. Paul we stopped at a Burger King. The boat show band was grousing about the price of the boat, believing it to be too high. There were some in my crowd who even suspected Menth of possible collusion with the mysterious Juul. I argued for Menth's virtue. I insisted that the hardware alone was worth the price. Not that I intended to acquire the boat for the hardware. My quickly developing new plan was to restore my father's utility, using the one I had started on the previous July as a parts boat, the new stem and stern bracings chalked up to experience or possibly removed to be used on Bud's boat.

"I'll go half," Bud said, once again demonstrating to

me his ability to communicate his various degrees of affection through boats. His financial participation was typical of the way he kept up his end of the bargain as my father.

We got it home the next weekend, the first weekend in April, and three-pointed it, the process by which a boat is blocked up at the two stern corners and under the keel about a third of the way back from the bow. As the boat gets blocked up the trailer can be wormed out from under it. It took most of another cold and rainy Saturday. Jennifer came out, looked at it, and said it was wrong—not the process of three-pointing it, of course, but its acquisition, its arrival, its presence.

"This boat isn't any good," she said. And then she went back into the house, her arms folded and her shoulders slightly hunched to suggest her disapproval.

I now had Bud's old boat in my garage and my virtually identical boat stored dry and clean three garages away. I was accumulating boats. It wasn't going over with Jennifer very well.

That night we towed the empty trailer back to Menth's. As we approached his place, Jennifer said she was going to be sick. She didn't get out of the car at Menth's. I quickly unhitched the trailer and said thank you to Menth, mumbling some excuse about having to get back on the road, and when I got back into the car Jennifer was crying. She handed the baby over the seat. It was raining, the wipers beating a rhythm to the silence in the car. I buckled the baby into the infant seat, and we started for home. Jennifer curled up in the back seat. She is never sick.

Going down the highway, she said she felt like she was going to die. Her voice was hollow and dry. Emily started to cry.

"Should we go to the hospital?" I said.

Jennifer didn't answer. When we got home I helped her into the house and she lay down on Emily's bed. She was shivering from a sudden fever, and her face was pale. I got the kids ready for bed, and then later, when her shivering stopped, I helped Jennifer get up the stairs and into our own bed.

She was sleeping soundly by midnight. She didn't bring it up the next day.

10 〰〰〰〰〰〰〰〰〰〰

Jennifer was instinctively correct about the arrival of Bud's boat into our life; in a kind of gypsylike way she usually is right, about many things. I don't think she had any inclination to introduce herself into the affairs of boats, but her brief and curious illness, had I paid attention to its deeper signals, was telling me to nurture what was mine and make my break with the past. Maybe it was easy for her, standing off to the side, to see only folly in resurrecting a boat, a lifeless thing at that.

"What's wrong with it being emotionally rewarding?" I asked her as she stood out in the garage on a cold spring day and agonized that I had reached too far with this project, two boats cluttering up our lives instead of one.

How could she answer my question? Our backgrounds were as different as water and land. The current minute of Jennifer's life was emotionally rewarding. She didn't need gimmicks. I was so colored and shaped by my past, by my time on the water, by my time in specific boats in specific emotional rituals, that I truly believed that the restoration of Bud's utility was a project pulsing with life, that I could somehow tie up the loose ends that I imagined to have with my father, or get from him, by resurrecting his boat, his approval and appreciation.

My father's boat had deteriorated beyond the point at which a reasonable man would have attempted to restore it. My other hull was in showroom condition compared with Bud's. Bud's boat was gone, leaving only a deceptive, ghostly trace of itself for me to try to touch. My dreams of what I wanted that boat to be had obscured its true condition. My memories didn't include the rain that had soaked it all the current spring and all the springs and winters of the past. Why, if you stopped to consider the extremes of weather it had withstood over the years—flood-producing rains in 1965, at least three so-called blizzards of the century between 1972 and 1985, temperatures swinging 100 degrees all year long, every year—it was a wonder the boat held together at all.

Once the hull dried out, I could put my finger through the sides and the decks and the bottom. I spent the precious month of April trying desperately to convince myself that the boat could be saved, but it could not be saved, short of carefully disassembling it and using its components, its salvageable frames, braces, planks, and stringers, to make patterns for a completely new boat.

Its bilge was as barren as a desert. Even extraordinarily difficult to get rid of bilge smells had been weathered out of wood that had been pounded by the rain and baked by the sun and frozen in the snows of long Minnesota winters.

I don't mean to limit the virtues of a bilge to its unmistakable odor. While it is true that even after years and years, even in a bilge as decomposed as mine, the smells set in motion the struggle to connect the present to the past, it is just as true that bilges are technically significant. Bilges are the souls of boats, to the extent that they reveal the framework of support so necessary to the life of the boat. They are important places to know. Like attics or basement storerooms, bilges show their eras, they mark their times, if only a body is willing to sift through the deposits of accumulated grime, of neglect.

There are practical reasons for going into a bilge and exploring around in it, and you probably don't need the emotional baggage that I haul along in order to enjoy an old boat. More people than not clean out bilges with industrial precision, throwing out everything that isn't fastened; they don't pay attention when they're down there rooting around.

From the practical standpoint, bilges are educational. A man shall never touch his hand to a cracked chine gusset, for example, or learn how to replace one, without first exposing the bilge and its maze of stringers, braces, and butt blocks, and hidden ruins of silt and grease. Bilges are terribly uncomfortable places, probably never meant to be explored by amateur hobbyists thirty, forty, and fifty years after being virtually sealed over at the factory with a subfloor and one or two removable pieces to provide access to the drive shaft packing nut and the battery.

I am equally as interested in what is not so easily understood, the powerful smells, the finding of old telltale clues to earlier generations, the notion that I somehow make connections to the past by laying my hands on the artifacts hidden in the crevices and recesses of time—and in the unreachable places, too. But this wasn't happening in my father's bilge.

The soul had gone out of that boat—his boat, not mine.

Around the first of May I officially gave up. I was in

the kitchen, fuming, having just come in from fuming in the garage. I needed to fume in front of an audience. I lit a cigarette and told Jennifer that I had had it, that I had made a mistake, and that I didn't know what to do about it.

"I have it in my mind that I should get the boat finished and running," I said, "that specific boat. But I can't. It's beyond me. And now I don't know what to do. I've blown the show this year, that's for sure. I've wasted a month on that piece of shit that is beyond repair. I thought everything could be fixed, but not everything can be fixed. Did you know that when you got sick?"

I gave her too many questions to answer and didn't wait for her to take on even one of them. She resisted saying that she had told me so. Hot-headed, I called Menth and read him the riot act for getting me involved in such a hopeless escapade. I called the newspaper and placed a classified ad. And then I went back to the garage and in my anger began to disassemble the boat, and not very carefully. I pried things loose. I ripped things off. I not-so-accidentally punched a hole in the bottommost transom board trying to remove the brass rod that connected the stern lifting ring to the keel. I removed every conceivable piece of hardware from the boat, and when at last I sold the scrapped hull—for $400 to a man from River Falls, Wisconsin—I included bits and pieces of hardware from the one I had started the previous summer, keeping everything from both boats that was remotely valuable so that the fellow didn't get much for his $400 except trouble.

Relief overcame me, not sadness, when it was hauled away down the alley, askew on its trailer and bouncing because so much weight was removed from it. It went down the alley the way a dog trots, a little sideways, a little sideways like that all the way to Wisconsin. It had come into my alley in an atmosphere of great hope, and it left as a number, serial number 17098. Relief overtook me because it wasn't my own, after all. It was Bud's through and through, and he had discarded it a long, long time ago for the not very significant reason that he had owned it long enough. I felt the emotional load lifted from me that implicit in its discovery was my responsibility to restore for my father memories that he might or might not want to have restored. The memories were of my choosing, I finally understood, not his, and the memories were entirely independent of the specific hull that generated them.

Beginning about two weeks after I sold it, incidentally, and for months afterwards, I saw an ad in some of the boat club newsletters for that same hull, as though the fellow who bought it from me concluded virtually in the act of towing it home that its repair was beyond him as well.

I soon enough rolled my own boat back into the garage, happy and relieved that I had not discarded it, for I might have impulsively done so in the excitement of having my father's genuine hull on hand. Working on that boat was a way to nurture my own, what was mine. It was a boat that I had discovered, however circuitously, acquired on my terms, and began working on in my garage. The boat came to me at a time in my life when its repair could even be said to parallel the repair of a child, which is not at all to ascribe to the boat any of the virtues of the healing child, except that, yes, all of us were suddenly back on the rails, steaming along, steaming along. Except for the ease with which she bruised, and that as a result of taking aspirin, Emily no longer had even a hint of Still's disease.

Time flew through the summer of 1985, good time, contented time. Many nights, after the new baby, Stephanie, was in bed, after the newspapers were read and the news was watched and bills were paid and real life was generally dispensed with, I'd get down from the highest shelf in the family room one of the *Bob Speltz Real Runabouts* volumes, of which there were four at the time, each of them as treasured and as wishful as seed catalogues or the *Baseball Encyclopedia*. At least they were treasured to me. Whenever one of them was in my hand, Jennifer accused me of once again studying our wedding pictures, which had the desired effect of making me sheepish. I would take a Speltz book over the wedding pictures any day, which I suppose was her point. Speltz books were the bibles of the hobby, less technical than historical—a rundown on virtually every North American manufacturer who ever built a wooden speedboat. While they were particularly comforting to read in the winter by a fire, with snow piling up at the window, they were especially useful in the summer, when I was more likely to be working on a boat and using Speltz photographs and text as reference. From *Real Runabouts*, volume I:

> Rounding out the 1938 utility offerings included a nice 17' with flat, folding windshield and nicely upholstered seats. No longer were utilities 'plain Janes' compared to the runabout.

Speltz, who lives on the shore of Fountain Lake in Albert Lea, Minnesota, created, in the mid-1970s, a self-perpetuating boat-book cottage industry. He had serious kidney problems. Every time he would go into the hospital, with a room overlooking his beloved Fountain Lake, he spent his time on dialysis researching his next book. In volume I, he gave such a cursory treatment to Chris Craft that it begged to be followed up in volume II, with "additional material applying to volume I." Same for volume II, so that there was fated to be a volume III. He was building a stairway to the moon with his books. Speltz's text begged to be edited, but that, too, was part of its charm. Personally, I would have eliminated the thousands of exclamation points, but then again, very few authors had ever put the makings for more raw and unabashed sentiment between hard covers. For example, I had looked at a picture on page forty-five of *Real Runabouts*, volume I—the Gar Wood section— a thousand times before I suddenly and quite gleefully one howling winter night sat bolt upright and said, "Hey, hey, wait a minute, that's Johnson Boat Works. That's my lake!"

The shot was taken from Johnson's, looking east, all the way to the east shore. I recognized the unmistakable curve of the lake around a neighborhood called Cottage Park, where on a narrow point of land a tree jutted out over the water in a way I suddenly recognized. There used to be a boat yard there when I was a boy, Amundson's, built hard to the shore and featuring a barnlike building with hayloft doors on the second floor that opened out over the lake in such a way that a boat could be lowered from the second floor to the water.

The photograph, not particularly remarkable, was probably taken in the 1930s. The boat in the picture was a 1927 twenty-six-foot Gar Wood three-cockpit runabout, one of the so-called Baby Gars. It was lashed to the dock at Johnson's. Its big square windshield was up. A ring buoy acted as a bumper between the boat's port side and the dock, which was edged with firehose. The dock looked like it would be hot to the bare foot.

The windshield, steering wheel, and front cockpit of another motorboat can be seen just ahead of the Gar Wood. Beyond the dock were five sailboats at their buoys, with a man standing on the deck of one of them, his weight on the pointed bow of the sailboat lifting the stern of it out of the water.

One July weekend, flushed with confidence, I lured fifteen people over and we did the unusual, if not the impossible. We turned the boat over. My crowd included a sportswriter, Shooter Walters, who once played for the Minnesota Twins and could still, at forty, throw a ball through a wall; two beverage truck drivers accustomed to hefting cases of soda; the three Johnson boys from just up the street, all of whom were as wiry as rodeo riders; Herb Lethert, who complained of a bad back and intended to act as foreman; the big bear from across the street, Endel; Joey the Actor; my immediate neighbor, Chet; as well as no fewer than five complete strangers. I am convinced that there are people in this world with a sixth sense for such adventure, shy people who materialize at the scenes of stuck cars and barn raisings and boats that need to be turned over.

Jennifer required our children to remain behind a locked fence, so that they could only peer into the alley, and then Jennifer said, "I really hope that all of you gentlemen with a back problem or a heart condition would either sign a waiver or leave the area." And then Jennifer and Keven closed the fence gate on themselves and stayed out of harm's way with their combined five children gathered around them, peeking through the slats in the gate.

We made two slings of rope, fore and aft, and picked the boat up off its trailer. Slowly, we shuffled in tiny, strained steps into the alley with it and rolled it over, setting down the starboard side on two upright but rimless automobile tires. The tires slowly collapsed under the weight of the hull, but there was enough manpower to guide the boat over and pick it up again before the hull ever even touched the ground. Then we shuffled it back into the garage and set it back down bottoms up, but not before I scampered under it and positioned a framework of concrete blocks as wide apart as the engine stringers.

Beers all around. We had started at noon, and it was supper time before the last of the strangers left, but not before I had recited all I ever knew about the history of Chris Craft.

If you want to get to the bottom of things, you must turn a boat over. I do not intend the obvious pun. Most amateurs, and probably most of the professionals, do not turn boats over. It is too difficult, if for no other reason than that it's difficult to get fifteen people over to your house on the same day. The only other way to accomplish a rollover is with a block-and-tackle assembly attached to roof beams, assuming the roof beams are more substantial than the two by fours in a normal garage and assuming the proprietor of a garage that's substantial enough to support the weight of a motorboat is not leery of block and tackle.

Most hobbyists and professionals lay on creepers underneath the boat, taking off as much old paint as possible and then caulking the seams by holding the caulking gun at an impossibly upright angle. By my way of thinking, too impractical. I wished to go all the way, in my renewed enthusiasm of getting back to working on my boat. My bottom work was incredibly convenient and satisfying. I filled a half-dozen grocery bags with melted-off paint, layer after layer after layer until at last I was down to the nostalgic and unmistakable old green. Then I sanded. Every morning for about two weeks I drove to work with a fine green-tinted mahogany dust on the hood and windshield of my car, dust that swirled away in the wind. I was able to make every bottom seam clean and uniform. I used epoxy to repair dents and restore a perfect edge on the chine, all the way around the perimeter of the boat. As with checking a newly sharpened skate blade, you could almost shave your fingernail on the edge I made for the chine.

Although it was becoming increasingly more popular and perfected, not to mention forgiven in serious antique boat show judging, I was philosophically opposed to fiberglassing the bottom. I aspired to the sound of wood, the flex of wood, the feel of wood, the shrinking and swelling of wood, characteristics that taken together authenticated the boat, made me a genuine partner to my forefathers in frustration. I remember my father, for example, being constantly consumed with the deviltry of a leaking boat. In swimming, he made it part of his exercises to examine the boat, running his hands along the bottom boards and around the stern, as though he intended to catch water in the act of breaking and entering one of his cotton-caulked seams. There was something almost touching in his grief, the way he literally, toward the end of his utility's life with him, had to put a clock on his time on the water to be sure to get back to the dock and the block and tackle before the boat grew heavy with its rolling load in the bilge. My mother always led the opposition forces who were convinced of either an impending explosion, on the occasion of catching even a faint whiff of gasoline, or imminent sinking, upon detection of the sloshing down below.

With the bottom sanded to bare wood, I painted on a sealer coat. The dry wood took it as a sponge takes water. Next, I masked each seam and ran the caulk in. Lastly, using a China bristle brush, I painted on three coats of the old cottage-awning green. The bottom looked new. I begged back approximately the same fifteen souls, and we picked the hull up, walked out into the alley, and turned it over in a reverse process. We shuffled back into the garage and set it down right-side up on the trailer, which was moved back into position.

Beers all around. It was fun; it was a neat thing to do just because it seemed so improbable to do it at all.

The show came and went without my entry. I was so absorbed in my own project that just a week after the show I remembered it in only isolated glimpses, brief mental film images of favorite boats. A Lake Okoboji, Iowa, boater named Al Mahaney showed up that year with a 1955 twenty-nine-foot Chris Craft Sportsman utility with twin engines. He called it *Acapulco*. Mahaney's boat was flawlessly and professionally restored. A dozen roses in a white cut-glass vase on the grated wood floor of his boat were reflected so deeply in the mahogany side paneling that the roses looked pressed under glass on the interior siding of the boat.

Moored across the dock from Mahaney's show winner (he won People's Choice, Best Classic Utility over twenty feet, and Best Classic Chris Craft) was a White Bear boat, Bill Reed's *Alice*. *Alice* was a 1931 twenty-six-foot Chris-Craft Model 111 runabout that had been converted into a sedan by Johnson's in the mid-1950s, with the construction of a hard top and the installation of a new Chrysler Imperial eight-cylinder engine. I knew Bill Reed; I had raced sailboats against Reed's son, Dean. And I knew *Alice*. It hung most of its life on the north shore of Manitou Island, a grand and imposing boat that was rarely out, save at dusk on a summer evening, its white hull knifing a narrow path through the water.

Reed had owned *Alice* since the late 1960s, and for

years he had tried to sell it. He bought it from one of the wealthy summer families on Manitou Island, one of the families that came out from Summit Avenue in St. Paul with steamer trunks in the spring and stayed until the shutters went up in September. Reed's efforts to sell *Alice* predated, by not more than a year or two, the sudden turnabout in preserving the old boats. Fortunately, rather than junk it, Reed built a boat house for it, long and narrow, and then took two years to restore *Alice* to as much of its original condition as he could while also maintaining the unique character that Johnson's gave the boat in its mid-fifties redux. That is, Reed returned the hull to its mahogany state. *Alice* had been a white-sided boat most of its life. Now, at the show, its long, narrow hull gleaming under a dozen coats of varnish, *Alice* looked like it belonged to a fleet of motorboats setting out to follow an America's Cup race, when twelve-meters were made of wood and flew cotton sails.

Reed found himself in demand as a storyteller at the show, probably because of *Alice*'s peculiar configuration. My favorite was the story of the bell under the dash. A heavy, brass bell was bolted under the dash. It was called a rough-weather bell. When children were out in *Alice* and the weather became rough enough to rock the boat into ringing the bell, they were to head for shore.

More spellbinding to most people was Reed's revelation that as recently as a few summers ago, he had missed finding, by exactly one day, the boat's original A-120 eight-cylinder, 825-cubic-inch, 250-horsepower engine, presumably in mint running condition, the boat's original decking over the engine compartment and all hardware (including chrome ventilators that looked as big as tubas compared with today's hardware). Johnson's had removed all the original equipment in the process of the sedan conversion. The engine, decking, and hardware sat on a trailer in a barn on Manitou Island, Reed learned after some detective work. Exactly one day before it occurred to Reed to inquire after the original equipment and to go after it, the trailer and its historic cargo had been removed to a landfill, dumped, and buried.

By early autumn of 1985 my hull was stained, the front deck was refastened, and a sealer coat had been applied. The boat was rapidly reaching the stage of almost exclusive reassembly. It was put away for the winter in the same stall as the previous year, needing only a new transom, a new rear deck, and a splashboard under the windshield to be structurally complete.

In the late autumn, the night before Thanksgiving, Pete Dunn came for the engine. In the bulb light of the garage, Dunn looked like the actor Gene Hackman. He backed his little boxy utility trailer up to the garage and we wrestled the engine onto the trailer bed, using a block and tackle that he hooked to the front of the trailer. I, of course, winced and turned my head from the task as we struggled the engine onto the trailer bed. It never took much to remind me of the broken winch handle.

Dunn was friendly and talkative, giving the impression that he could handle anything. I didn't think I could be lucky enough to find another Ray, but that's what I thought, hot damn, another Ray. It was cold out, and as black as a moonless night could be. The wind rustled dry leaves down the alley. It was cold enough that we didn't even build up a sweat moving the engine. I gave Dunn a check for $500, the balance of an additional $500 due upon completion—around Christmas, Dunn said. He said he would return to me a complete and perfectly running engine.

His name came to me by way of the boat club grapevine.

11

IN MARCH 1986, the temperature shot surprisingly into the seventies and the snowmelt ran like floodwater. There wasn't any warning. One day it was cold, with sooty snow in the north-side shadows of buildings, and the next day the birds were singing and the air smelled fresh and warm, a lake smell on the air. So many people suddenly appeared out of doors, running and walking and riding bicycles, that you would have thought a large trapdoor had opened to free us all from the storm cellar of winter.

The boat got sprung from its storage and moved regally down the alley and back into my garage on Easter Sunday, March 30, record early, and I needed record early to make the show in August. It was my second spring to withdraw the boat from storage, but now the boat was nearing completion. I drafted the able-bodied males from Easter brunch at my aunt's in St. Paul, and together we pushed the boat down the alley, our feet slipping in the sandy residue of winter.

A variety of odd jobs and necessary tasks had been

accomplished over the winter. After trying local watch repairmen and speedometer-building shops, I sent the instruments away to an instrument restorer named Pat Powell, working out of Chicago. Powell advertised his services in the fliers and magazines devoted to antique boating. About two weeks after I sent him my fragile parcel he called me, wondering if I had wanted him to attempt to heighten the dark silhouettes etched into the chrome oval plate that surrounded the instrument cluster. They were the silhouettes of Chris Crafts racing around bell buoys on the Detroit River, with that faint cold November look of industrialization on the shoreline in the background. Because Powell said his methods should be considered experimental and therefore risky, we decided to leave the oval plate alone. I could see the boats racing around the buoys plain enough.

After I successfully removed the throttle lever and the horn button from the steering column, I couldn't for the life of me pull the steering wheel off its shaft. The throttle and horn mechanisms were integral to the steering column. The thin brass throttle rod running down the inside of the steering shaft joined a clamping assembly on the back side of the steering box. A solid brass rod ran from the clamping assembly on the back side of the steering box to a clump of pivoting hardware, and from there another brass rod ran along a stringer back to the engine and hooked onto the carburetor. The entire assembly was as mysterious to me as a glockenspiel.

Even though the steering wheel was deeply cracked and uniformly faded, its hub destroyed in a pattern of fissures and thin, spidery cuts, I still feared ruining the wheel further by forcing it off the shaft. I needed to save the wheel, to have it restored. I did not save the wheel from Bud's utility, the curiously painted white wheel. It was in approximately the same condition of ruin as his hull.

I ended up taking the wheel, its shaft, and the steering box to an automobile restoration outfit experienced in wheel pulling. I also presented to them my collection of springs, snap rings, washers, clamps, grommets, horn button, and throttle lever that I had accumulated when I disassembled the apparatus.

"What is this," they asked me, "a prank?"

"Hey, come on," I said, "these things are automotive."

My calls around the country to various steering wheel restorers scared me off a wheel restoration. The costs were prohibitive. Any money that I spent on the boat came from a so-called boat fund that I dribbled $25 and $50 into here and there, mostly spare change from speaking engagements; the fund was never healthier than about $300 at any given time. I kept my receipts and tried to be orderly about it, too, but the collection got to be as thick and tattered and thumbprinted as a parts book on a machine shop city desk.

I ended up buying a virtually identical four-spoke mid-1930s Ford wheel from the automobile shop, plain and basic black. Chris Craft used automotive wheels, mostly Fords before World War II and then beautiful Chrysler-Plymouth wheels in the late 1940s and into the 1950s. Some of those Plymouth wheels showed a schooner under sail behind the plastic hub.

The plating and polishing work was done at three different shops, all of them smelling acrid and looking environmentally dangerous with dip tanks and a powdery metallic dust everywhere, not to mention the presence outside one of them of a surly old German shepherd with his ribs showing, circling on a patch of dirt that he had worn into a smooth ring. One of the shops, Quality Plating and Polishing, Inc., was just down Cayuga Street from a ramshackle place called Bears (no apostrophe), an honest-to-God Harley-Davidson repair and custom parts shop (I found in the phone book) right in the middle of St. Paul. Bear, said to be a former Hell's Outcast, worked out of a garage set back on the property. The property was posted with rusty tin signs that gave the business hours.

Quality Plating was in a cinder-block building with unpainted wood trim. The people there did superb work, but they were so expensive that I stopped bringing pieces there and found two other shops with lower rates, both of those shops in the same near-north neighborhood built around Oakland Cemetery in the north end of St. Paul. It was ancient all around; the cemetery opened in 1853 and the homes around it were small and old, once primarily the flats of railroad workers.

Over the winter, in the basement, I took the tongue-and-groove engine doghouse apart and put it back together again, but not before I had soaked most of the pieces in the bathtub. Doghouses, so called because they are just about the size of conventional doghouses, come apart nicely. Neglect and weather had caused so much warping that I took each individual piece and soaked it, weighing it down with a cement block. There was a two-week stretch there when bath hour every evening was preceded by removing bricks and boards from the tub, only to plant them again after the bath hour. The first appearance of my boards was unannounced, so that when an unsuspecting Jennifer went into the bathroom to start the baths one night, she got a quick peripheral glimpse of something trapped under the water and let out a scream. I had to come running from the basement to explain.

While I was down there rooting around in the basement, I made a Christmas present. When I said I kept everything from Bud's hull that could possibly be kept, I wasn't exaggerating. I cut a square patch of wood from one of the transom boards I had saved from his hull, sanded it, stained it, and varnished it, to make a wall plaque. To the refinished wood I attached the brass Chris Craft identification tag that I had removed from the underside of the doghouse in his boat. Stamped into the plate was his boat's serial number, 17098, plus the manufacturer's instructions for maintenance and the Algonac mailing address for acquiring parts.

Beneath the brass plate I screwed the postwar Chris Craft emblem that had been screwed to his dash.

The engine that was to have been delivered by Christmas hadn't yet arrived in the spring. I developed a curious relationship with Pete Dunn, whom I hadn't laid eyes on since that cold, windy night in November. Dunn and I didn't have much telephone contact. I rarely reached him. He rarely returned calls. On occasions when I did reach him he admitted running into an obstacle or two or three, and I always thought him to be telling the truth. After all, I had no urgent need for the arrival of the motor. In fact, I wasn't ready for the motor and wished to time its arrival so that the day Pete Dunn showed up with it, I could lower it directly onto the engine stringers and bolt it down; it didn't bother me, or scare me, or even alert me to the notion of being scared when Dunn routinely wasn't ready to deliver the goods.

Of greater urgency to me, with the boat back in my garage, was the remaining carpentry—the new stern and rear deck, the new floorboards, the seat framing, and the splashboard under the windshield. By salvaging the pieces of the old seats, I was able to give Ray enough pattern to make out of new wood, a facing piece for the rear seat—to a passenger in the sitting position, the piece behind bended knee to the floor—as well as a rear seat back. The pattern for the splashboard was Bud's old splashboard. The standard utilities had no windshield; the splashboard presumably had exactly that purpose, to deflect water. On the Deluxe models, the bottom edge of the flat, folding windshield sat atop the splashboard. The salvaged splashboard was too rotted to use, thus the need to make one from scratch. Because I was going to use the windshield from my father's boat, his splashboard was the logical pattern.

What was quickly taking shape was the development of my restored hull, complemented by virtually every piece of hardware off of hull 17098—a hybrid of function and sentiment. My hull, despite needing urgent and strategic replacement of the oak stem and transom bracing, was nevertheless more solid than Bud's old hull, which had become cardboardy. His hardware perfectly replaced precisely what was missing on my sounder hull—most specifically the windshield; I had seen flat, folding windshields advertised for as much as $700 without brackets.

I also intended to use his bow light, his rope chocks, his lifting rings, his shift lever, his decorative bollard from his front deck, even the small flat chrome plate that backed the starter button on his boat. Everything that I would touch in the operation of my boat would have been touched by him and by his people before him. A laying on of hands that would connect me to generations of my family that I didn't even know.

Ray began to see the larger picture, which I think he might have purposely shut his eyes to in the beginning. I suspect that the pieces he had to make initially were so difficult—I remain convinced that he didn't want to make them—that it prevented him from embracing the emotional significance of the project. Ray was so precise, so literal in the beginning of our partnership, that I had to be careful to explain to him that a dent or a gouge in a piece of wood was merely a dent or a gouge and was not to be incorporated into whatever new piece he was making—he was that precise.

By the new spring, Ray's hand was so evident everywhere in the boat that I believe he began to anticipate the boat's completion as much as I did.

It constituted a peculiar ethical dilemma. Was I really doing the work, or was Ray? We decided that I was, principally because Ray and I had reached an arrangement in which he considered me his apprentice. I helped him, although I deferred to him in matters in which the principles of, say, geometry might have been applied to our task. It was beyond my comprehension, for example, how to measure a flat board that was dramatically curved when it was fastened across the stern.

What a good stretch of time that was in the early spring with the air still sharp and cool, building out there in the garage, the shop, watching Ray study a piece of wood and pull back from it in a demonstration of farsightedness. Monday was our day, the rest of the week spent planning what we would accomplish on Mondays. Ray always wore a dark-blue baseball-style cap with a red patch on the crown that said Aggregate Cemstone Concrete. He sported the visor at an upward tilt. His glasses rode low on the tip of his nose. He wore a work apron over his poplin jacket, in which he kept stubs of pencil that he fished for among the crumbs of sawdust that ended up there.

The stern of the boat, which we were replacing, was backed into the garage. I hung the trouble light on a hook above the stern or held it for Ray if he needed specific light. He was not shy about asking for light or lax in taking care with his tools.

"You can't beat the right tools," Ray said.

Ray used a hand drill. He could have used a power screwdriver, but he used an old ratchet-style driver, up and down, like a pump. Rather than use a power sander, he did his rough sanding with eighty-grit paper wrapped around a block of wood. He was all feel, hands on, his fingers studying the work. The wood felt good to Ray, and he never abused the majesty of wood by applying power to it when the touch of his finger would do. In photographs I took of Ray installing the new stern deck and the new transom boards, he looks studious but completely happy and at ease. He worked nonstop, through and through, all out.

"Ray, can I get you anything?"

"No, Joe, I'm fine."

"Soup or something?"

"No."

He never went to the bathroom. When he was rolling, he was rolling. Maybe once, twice a week, he would ask for a tall glass of water and then mention that in the days when he was considered a fine amateur softball player, he never drank much on a hot day, maybe one cold beer when the game was over, to settle the dust. He drank the water in one pull and then resumed work, instructing me in a variety of principles, chief among them that wood is forgiving.

"You can make mistakes with wood," Ray said, "the wood forgives you and you can keep working right through the mistake, like with the stem, when we put the stem in and the first bolt through missed the mark. We were able to save that by redrilling."

One day at his house I asked Ray out of the blue what was important in life. I had taken to bringing the pieces to him and picking them up, to lighten the feeling of vague guilt I had developed for dragging him into the job. We were hanging around his garage, where he had cut me all new floorboards. He had just finished cleaning and tuning up one of his sons' power lawnmowers; he was always doing something for one of his two boys, both of whom were electricians. Now the lawnmower was out in the sun, and Ray had just finished wiping it clean with a cloth that he kept in the back pocket of his work jeans.

"Family," Ray answered my question. "Making sure they're taken care of."

I waited for more. What I wanted from Ray, I suppose, was some reassurance that I wasn't just pissing time away. Only loosely could I convince myself that boat restoration was a hobby. It had become, at best, an impractical obsession.

"You're not in a saloon, Joe," Ray said.

"Excuse me?"

"Lots of guys in saloons, Joe," Ray said.

"You mean newspaper guys?" I said.

"Guys in general," Ray said.

It wasn't the first time he had made an allusion to how my time might have been wasted. I think there is a generation of Americans to whom a drink constitutes slackness. My mother-in-law often said the same thing to me, responding to light complaints from my wife and children that I was spending too much time with the boat.

"Well, he's not hanging around in bars," she would say, God love her.

It is not necessarily a generation opposed to alcohol, but it is a generation so impressed with the urgency to be always working that any threat to the job would be viewed as worse, obviously, than the job itself, no matter what the job.

"But the money you're spending," Ray said. "Oooooboy."

Ray was sly, thrifty. He knew the prices of board feet of lumber and was always distressed at having to pay for lumber that had knots in it. The piece of oak from which he made the stem cost $50. To Ray—whom I suspect of having a fortune salted away, carefully recorded in his ledgers—it might as well have been $5,000. The only thing I could do was remind Ray what the same project would cost in the hands of a professional, taking care to make sure Ray knew I understood that he was a professional.

"I wouldn't be doing it if it wasn't for you," I said.

12 〰〰〰〰〰〰〰〰〰〰

MID-JUNE 1986, and still no engine. Slight panic, manifesting itself by short temper and the occasional skipped heartbeat. I imagined a clock ticking and I began to feel the pressure of my arbitrary deadline—the show, on the second weekend in August. I filled out the show's registration application the day I received it in the mail. The same day I sent along my check for thirty-five dollars, reserving my dock space, making me an entrant. After all these years I was going to have a boat in the show, and very nearly the boat I always wanted to have in it, certainly a boat that I could tell stories about to the curious souls who would gather around my slip and ask me the same questions I had asked so many others.

"Well, when I brought it home the stem fell smack onto the garage floor . . . I'm not kidding . . . broke into three pieces, it was so rotted . . . yup, same boat my dad had when I was a boy . . . in fact, we found my dad's actual boat; well, it's a long story if you have the time."

I was planning to bring pictures. It would constitute

an enchantment to boat fans to see the condition of the boat when I started. Not many boats in the shows were as rough as mine, and not many amateurs went to the lengths I was going. The thought of winning an award didn't occur to me. I just wanted to be there, futzing around in it, coiling ropes, wiping the windshield to a sparkle with a diaper, sitting in the sun in the back seat drinking beer, the lord of my buoyant domain. Maybe get lucky, too, watch a man and a boy approach me through the thicket of tall, tanned legs on the dock, the man and boy stopping dumbstruck in front of my boat saying:

"We had one just like that."

And then watch the wheels of their memories start turning.

Varnishing began in June, coinciding with Bud's developing a staph infection in his left arm after surgery that was intended to restore manipulation to the arthritically crippled fingers in his left hand.

It was getting to be a race with a perverse irony; the closer the boat came to completion, the worse my father got. I seriously doubted whether he would be able to make the show. The staph infection kept him hospitalized most of June and into July. When I went to visit him it was like every other hospital visit we ever had, reasonably formal conversation in which was hidden, via the code language of boats, exchanges of emotional information—How are you? I'm pulling for you. Everything all right in your life, your work?—that might just as easily have been asked outright if we had ever gotten into the habit of straightforwardness. He was hospitalized during a spell of hot weather, so that despite the air-conditioning in his room, the sun was a hot presence behind the gauzy curtains that puffed out from the cool-air vents at the base of the windows, motes of dust riding the skirts of the puffed curtains. The room smelled closed-up, the way our house in St. Paul smelled in the 1950s, during the summers when we lived at the cottage.

"Varnishing is starting," I'd tell him.

God, how I hated hospitals. Emily had been swallowed up by the size of her hospital bed, her aloneness in the room. Hospitalized in the fullness of summer, just like Bud. Bud, though, filled the room.

"What about the engine?" he'd say.

I hated the smells, the boredom, the habit that even well-meaning nurses have of speaking condescendingly to grown men and women, introducing *we* into every sentence. The patronization isn't so bad with a child, especially one lying there in a delirium. It killed Bud to be talked to sweetly, too sweetly. It caused him to arch his eyebrows and do double takes of mock pain behind the nurse's back.

"The engine isn't done yet," I'd say, pretending unconcern. "But I'm not worried, because I really don't need it yet. In fact, I'd like to get it as late as possible. That way I can put it immediately into the boat the day it arrives."

"I'd be worried about that engine," he said.

"Well, I'm not," I said, knowing very well that the engine's absence was driving me up the wall. "It'll get here."

"I never was any good at varnishing," he said. "I know that you lay it on." He made a laying on motion with his right hand, the unbandaged one, but it was puffy, the knuckles swollen. "Conditions have to be just perfect. I varnished our old Sportsman in the driveway, remember that? Every kid in the block helped on that one."

"That boat looks great in pictures," I said. "I remember it looking great."

"Not up close it didn't," he said.

A freshly starched nurse brought him a juice drink and said, "How are we feeling?" She put the juice on his bed tray. He took a drink of juice from the white styrofoam cup. He required two hands to hold the cup, two stiff, clumsy hands that gave him the look of a beggar drinking hot soup. He was not able to shave in the hospital as often as he normally did. The stubble of beard was showing silver on his face and dozens of small red veins had become visible on his cheeks.

The boat that succeeded Bud's utility was the twenty-two-foot Sportsman—The Boat That Broke Loose from the Car. That one had angleworms in the bilge. We discovered them down there in a petrified state, in dried clumps of black dirt. Before we got it, that boat saw duty at a fishing resort in northern Wisconsin. The angleworms spoke less of neglect and more of an era when fishing resorts were so impossibly quaint that I could imagine the lodge keeper taking the whole gang of his customers out and giving each of them a paper cup full of worms.

My father, the same man who would routinely throw away most normal references to his past, including winter carnival memorabilia, bequeathed to me during the restoring of my utility his file of correspondence pertaining to his purchase of the Sportsman. He did not for a moment intend to suggest that the documents were important or that they constituted any revelation that I might find useful. In fact, he gave them to me as if to say, "Here, you evidently are amused by this old stuff; look at how useless it is."

It was not at all useless. It was instructive, if for no other reason than that it showed the dramatic results of inflation in just a little more than twenty years. The file, found while he was cleaning out an office drawer, contained seven documents in all, including a bill of sale dated September 13, 1962, or about a month after he must have given over the utility to get himself square at Johnson's. The bill of sale was signed by one Warren Le Noue, on the sales department staff at Minnetonka Boat Works. In the agreement, Bud agreed to pay $850 for one "used 22' Chris Craft Sportsman powered with 115 hp Chrysler engine and equipment; folding top and cradle."

Also included in the file was a storage bill, dated December 27, 1962, for $86.90, a storage rate of $3.95 per foot. The boat was located in shed 3, storage number 405. The boat's equipment was inventoried and included keys, a paddle, a battery, two tie ropes, a stern pole, a spotlight, two running lights, a fire extinguisher, five cushions, one folding canvas top, and a cradle.

The remaining documents were the correspondence between my father and Minnetonka regarding work that the boat works intended to perform. Actually, they were pitching for the work. On Minnetonka Boat Works stationery with a border of blue-green waves, Warren Le Noue wrote:

> I went over your 22' Sportsman with our service manager and the following is what we believe you will want done.
> Remove all exterior varnish, sand, stain, & varnish 3 coats. $320.00
> Sand, caulk where needed and paint bottom. $40.00
> Remove and straighten rudder. $15.00
> Check shaft alignment—if new shaft needed, install. $34.50
> Sand and varnish inside of boat. $70.00
> I think this covers the work we spoke about over the telephone, so I will wait for a confirming letter as to what work you want done.
>
> Yours truly,
> Warren Le Noue

My father wrote back on February 8, 1963:

Attention: Warren Le Noue:

In answer to your letter concerning work to be done on my 22' Sportsman.

I would like to have your company remove and straighten rudder and check shaft alignment—if new shaft needed, install it.

I believe I shall attempt the other repairs myself.

Yours truly,
J. Henry Soucheray.

The joke around our family when I was growing up was that we didn't know what our father did for a living. We knew only that he went downtown, dressed impeccably, to an office building in the very heart of St. Paul, on Fourth Street between Cedar and Wabasha. There, he was "in business," or "a businessman." Nothing quite so demonstrates the nature of his public life as the letter to Warren Le Noue, particularly the polite and almost elegant last line—"I believe I shall attempt the other repairs myself."

J. Henry, as he was known in his circles of commerce and clubs, was the vice president of the St. Paul Abstract and Title Guarantee Company. If we did not know precisely what that was or what he did, we had the evidence around our house of the company's scratch pads, rulers, pens, and letter openers. The company was started by his grandfather, who literally stood at a lectern before the turn of the century and hand-wrote the title deeds to virtually all of the residential property in St. Paul. As near as

I came to understanding it, my father's firm not only produced the title to a specific piece of property but also vouched for its legitimacy. Because such work invariably drew into his circle bankers, attorneys, lenders, and brokers, it was also the joke around our house that my father knew everyone in St. Paul. Everyone. On the occasions when I went downtown to the doctor— conveniently enough Bud's only brother, my uncle Phil—and stopped to see my father, he could not walk twenty feet down the sidewalk without a salutation to one of his lodge brothers in business: "Hello there, Jack, nice to see you."

When we would go to a St. Paul Saints hockey game in the old St. Paul Auditorium, it seemed to me that he knew every soul we passed from the parking lot to our seats in the arena.

"Is this the youngster, Henry?" one of his cronies would ask.

"Why, yes," my father always said, formally, "I'd like you to meet my son, Joe."

I came to learn that he didn't necessarily know how to assemble an abstract of title or issue a certificate of title, but he knew that his company could, and he made it his business to be sure that every user of the service was convinced of that fact. His motto for success was simple: "Do business with your friends. The more friends you have, the better your business."

I felt curiously important in the company of such hale fellows, so well met, on those occasions when we walked together through St. Paul in the early 1960s. It was easy to see that he was well liked, respected, known. I didn't need any evidence to know it myself, but based on his public recognitions, others considered him to be an honorable man as well, and honest.

*   *   *

I'd stay thirty, forty minutes in the hospital—usually my mother was there, leafing through a magazine while we talked about boats—and then I'd leave, always pretending that I wasn't concerned, pretending that because his condition was so obviously under control it didn't merit concern. I suppose it reflects the measure of our deceptive tricks that I should say I assumed his condition was under control. His condition was terrible. He looked terrible. He sounded terrible.

I had the boat to turn to, Little League, the recuperated Emily, a baby, Jennifer. I had youth all around me, the hard physical activity of young lives. Refreshed, I'd return to the hospital the next day, only to find it uncomfortable again, the heat making it through the curtain, the hospital smelling sour in the daytime sunshine, a game show or soap opera on television somewhere in the distance, the bothersome sounds of the game show host, the lovelorn.

"You say you lay on the varnish," I said, settling in for another visit. I'd routinely offer news of my children, who just as routinely visited him, but if we ever were in danger of not having anything to talk about, or if I imagined the silences between us too prolonged or awkward, there was always the boat to talk about, the varnishing process.

"Yes, lay it on," he said, making that motion with his good hand.

Most amateurs and hobbyists are unskilled craftsmen and will go to great lengths not to have to make a stem, but will spend hours and hours learning varnishing techniques. I really kept my ear to the ground when it came to varnishing. I opened myself up to hundreds of sources of information and dockside talk and then threw out what I didn't like, so that when it came time for me to actually start laying it on, I paid homage to a good half-dozen principles of application.

It starts with preparing the room in which the varnishing is to be done. I empty the garage completely and then hose it down—rafters and everything—and put it back together again. Serious varnishing requires at least a preliminary cleaning of the shop, lest you end up laying varnish over the motes and specks of sanding dust from six months, a year back down the road.

On the day of an actual session, you anticipate everything possible before going at it. For example, get the bicycles out of the garage in case a child comes looking for one. Then, close the big garage door, arrange clamp lights to the wall studs to illuminate the hull sides—boats about to be varnished demand better and more consistent lighting than even aging and egotistical theatrical stars—turn on the radio, bat the brush, take a deep, meditative breath. In perfect theory, the boat would have been vacuumed the previous day. The hull may be tack-wiped a final time, but not vacuumed on a varnishing day. Vacuum exhaust would stir too much dust. I would have attempted to explain this curious process to Jennifer, but I do believe she would have called in the white coats; she rarely lets me forget that when we first got married I saw no need to even own a vacuum, much less did either of us ever envision the day when I would use one as an instrument of precision.

Lastly, you go outside the garage and hail a child, Andy or Emily, and you tell them to go to the faucet and when you yell, to turn on the water. Then you put your hands on your knees and tell yourself that you are going into a big game and you had best concentrate. Then you yell:

"Turn on the hose!"

The water rushes along the trail of the hose, filling

it, and when the water appears from the end—no nozzle, mind you—you turn, lay the hose on the garage floor, and soak the floor, dust-proofing it, snaking the hose every which way until the entire floor of the garage is wet and sloppy underfoot, as though after a hard rain. Then you go back to the door and yell:

"Shut her off!"

And then you disappear from the world, closing the service door gently behind you to the now-muffled summer sounds outside. Some guys go fishing in the wilds of Canada or tour Yellowstone on a driving vacation. I disappear into the garage, the faces of Andy and Emily sometimes pressed up to the window as though I had boarded a train that was slowly leaving the station I would let them in the garage during varnishing, but I don't think the fumes would be good for them. Truth be told, I don't want them to accidentally touch the boat, or worse, sneeze.

All preparatory work has been completed. A proper amount of varnish is now poured into a strainer in a paper cup, the cup to be thrown away since no varnish will be returned to the can. And then I have at it, in the brightness of brilliant artificial light, a side of the boat at a time, never two sides in one session.

Countless articles have been written about the art of varnishing, and the only shred of truth in any of them is the notion of the task being called an art. It is the most difficult and yet most rewarding job in the process of bringing an old boat back from the graveyard of weathered boards. What the articles don't say—although they make an attempt—is that each man, woman, and child who ever holds a varnishing brush has to discover his or her own technique. There is no right, universal way of laying on varnish, but there is a key concept; it gets laid on, it doesn't get painted.

Varnishing must be done alone. It strengthens the bond between owner and boat. The aloneness fosters pleasant daydreaming; the time spent heightening the craftsmanship of an ancient hull actually strengthens and deepens nostalgic feelings for it, so that as the varnish begins to illuminate the hull sides, the memories become clearer. I usually varnished to a cassette tape I was stuck on, Jim Capaldi's "One-Man Mission." I was in heaven during varnishing. I loved the escape, the residual physical aches and pains of labor, from being in a crouched position, from the consistent and patient stroking of the brush. I loved accomplishing something physically skillful, being lost like that in my own world with no deep thoughts. My children had no reasonable convictions, no evidence, really, that I actually worked for a living. My schedule was too easy come and too easy go. They didn't read the newspaper, to see that I was employed. Once, watching me halfheartedly scraping paint from our basement walls, Andy said, "You know, Dad, this is the first job you've ever had."

To my children, varnishing was a demonstration of work.

By some act of God or some curious biological circuitry, if there is a distinction, I am good at varnishing. By rights I shouldn't be. I think of good varnishers as having patient, Type B behavior, pipe smokers, like Ray (even though he doesn't smoke). Ray, in fact, hates varnishing and absolutely refuses to refinish the cradles and bookshelves and flower boxes he is forever building on consignment.

I am a compulsive, impatient, generally loud and anxious Type A character all the way. But I am good at varnishing. Perhaps I am lulled into a drugged state by the fumes, although it is more likely that I reach an agreement with my inner being to apply myself to the task because I know it is the one job that is guaranteed to generate a response.

The Chris Craft That Broke Loose from the Car, the twenty-two-foot Sportsman, was, in fact, varnished in our driveway. Worse, from an artistic standpoint, my father allowed every kid in the neighborhood to help—as much evidence as I can produce that in their eras such boats were merely boats and not precious things. It seemed like a dozen of us were crawling around that boat, laying on varnish in the wind. The wind blew bits of sand and leaves. The bits of sand and leaves clung to the sticky varnish. From a distance the hull looked good. Up close it looked like neighborhood kids had varnished it in the wind.

When I varnish the port side of my boat I start at the bow and work back, opposite on the other side, because I am right-handed and always find it easiest to varnish while moving slowly to my right. Runs are avoided merely by gently stroking the varnish until it ceases to run, or drape, feathering it out at the end of a stroke where the next application will begin. A dollop of Penetrol extends the varnish life and makes it set up more slowly than it would if it was applied full strength.

From mid-June to mid-July, I conducted a full-fledged varnishing concert no fewer than sixteen times, until the hull received eight coats. One day I stopped. Perfection might have been achieved by giving the hull a ninth coat. The problem with that notion was the inevitable feeling that perfection might have been achieved with a tenth coat and then an eleventh and then a twelfth. It could have gone on forever, becoming my life's work.

13 ∿∿∿∿∿∿∿∿∿∿∿∿

HARRY ZEMKE, HIS WIFE, LINDA, and their two daughters were waiting in their yard in a peculiar kind of suburban American Gothic pose when my brother Paul and I arrived at Harry's with the boat, the trailer hooked to Paul's pickup truck. As I had done in my college years, Paul had purchased cheap summer transportation, in Paul's case a 1972 Chevrolet pickup truck that was so rusted I could not understand how the body still clung to the frame. (I commuted to higher learning in a 1954 Ford Mainliner with a decal of a flame-spitting rocket ship on its trunk.) The back bumper of Paul's truck was so high that the boat appeared to have been dragged from St. Paul to Zemke's place in White Bear township, north of White Bear, where the last few homes of suburbia are up against rolling farm fields. Paul and I got out, mirror images of each other, the first and last of the brothers and sisters, separated by nearly twenty years.

Pulling into the dirt driveway behind us were my aunt Rita, her two daughters, and my Emily, all of whom got out and stretched in the hot driveway, saying "That's a relief," probably referring to getting away from our house in St. Paul as much as the long trip out. It was crazy there for a while back home. Rita had driven over to see the finished boat in my garage and had stumbled into our loud and profane preparations to get the boat the hell out to Harry's.

"And you," Jennifer had said, taking Rita by the arm, "will follow them out to White Bear because this trailer might not make it."

Rita never did get a word in. She got back into her car, felt around the bottom side of the steering column to engage the flashers and then followed us out. It might have been a funeral procession, because we went that slowly, and for part of the journey, before he peeled off for home at the city limits, we also were accompanied by Jennifer's brother, Steve, who raced ahead to each intersection on his big Honda Gull Wing motorcycle.

We were a frazzled crew when at last we arrived at Harry's, damp, dusty, road weary, our joints creaking and aching.

Harry took all of us in and said, "Linda, get us a beer."

Linda was deeply tanned, with high, handsome cheekbones and raven-black hair. Her children were dark, too, bronzed from a summer outdoors. Dust made chalky patterns on their bare feet. Linda melted away as fluidly as Wodehouse's Jeeves, into the shadows of the open garage. There was a plastic cooler on the floor of the garage. We could hear tinkling in the shadow of the garage when Linda gathered up the bottles, and then she melted into view again, silently.

"Have a beer, Joe," Harry said.

I swallowed mine in one long pull. Paul did the same.

It had taken longer than an hour to make the twenty miles out from town. We crawled along back roads, fearful of the stern scraping the road. It was hot in the cab of the pickup. We hadn't talked much.

Harry walked around the boat. He looked like Jerry Garcia of the Grateful Dead. Harry wore cutoff blue jeans, a T-shirt, and a cap. His stomach was big, but he carried it on a big frame. His black hair was scraggly and stuck out from under the cap. His sideburns were country long and he had a mustache. He laughed easily, a high-pitched giggle with a lot of air behind it. His family always seemed to frame him , move around behind him. If Harry was on one side the boat, Linda and the girls were over there, hanging back. I'd make him thirty-five, thirty-six.

"Linda, get Joe and Paul another beer," Harry said. "Please."

"I'll get it," I said. It was Sunday, July 27, two weeks before the show. The day had a strong Sunday feel to it, one of those rare summer days when people stay home for a change, when they don't pull their boat to the lake or play softball or go to a picnic. Harry's big fiberglass Rinker speedboat was parked crossways in the three-stall garage. There are only a couple of days every summer like it, when people in Minnesota stop exhausting themselves with frantic summer activity and actually just poke around home for a day, enjoying a slower pace. I felt as though we had intruded. Seeing Harry and his family waiting for me in their yard like they were made me feel guilty about robbing them of one of these special days.

"No problem," Linda said, melting away again. She seemed cheerfully used to getting beer.

"Damn, you did a nice job, Joe," Harry said, running his hand along the hull. "God, I love these old Chris Crafts."

The boat looked spectacular in the sunshine. The

chrome gleamed. The sun played on the varnished hull, making the varnish look deep and golden. It was set off by the white waterline and the cottage-awning-green bottom.

"You could win with this boat," Harry said.

"Did you ever win with yours?" I asked him.

Harry had entered a Chris Craft Riviera in the show a few summers back.

"I enjoyed the brunch," Harry said, thumping his belly.

I laughed.

"I think it's politics," Harry said, meaning the way the boat shows are won and lost. "I didn't win."

I told him I hadn't thought of winning. But in the sunshine, with two beers taking the edge off the trip out, I thought of winning. I thought the boat looked as good as any I had seen. I thought it looked fantastic; I had surprised myself with what I had done. Now all I had to do was get it running.

"So what's with the engine?" Harry said. "You sounded pretty uptight when you called yesterday."

I told him the story, the whole truth, nothing but the truth, so help me God. I told him everything, hoping to win him over. The story took time. I told him first about the hull, how it was a hull I started working on two summers ago, in July of 1984, and then, in the spring of 1985, how I found my father's old boat, his precise boat. Harry jumped in at that point to tell me that his Riviera had been discovered in similar circumstances, outdoors, the boards weathered barn-gray

I told Harry how unsalvageable my father's hull turned out to be and how the hull I kept needed so much carpentry, the stern braces and the new oak stem. I told Harry about Ray and finally I told him about Pete Dunn, who had come so highly recommended and yet remained so enigmatic.

"Every weekend since April," I told Harry, "Dunn promised to deliver the engine. At first I didn't worry when he never showed up because I wasn't ready for the engine. But then the entire month of June went by. I got worried. He kept coming up with excuses."

Finally, I told Harry, on the day before, Saturday, July 26, Pete Dunn showed up in my alley. He was supposed to have arrived Friday night, but by midnight I gave up waiting for him and I spent a restless night in bed, listening to the buses on Cretin Avenue down the block, listening to the softer sounds of night in the city, the rustling of leaves, kids shooting off leftover firecrackers. I didn't sleep.

I knew the minute I saw the engine that I was going to have problems. It was in the same boxy utility trailer that Dunn had hauled it away in on that cold night in November, the night before Thanksgiving. The trailer was littered with empty quart oilcans, pieces of timber, patches of canvas, lifting chains, two bald tires. Dunn had spray-painted the engine, but evidently so quickly and so carelessly that brass parts and rubber parts were discolored with a telltale blue overspray. The generator and starter looked like they hadn't been removed from the engine; nuts and bolts were rusty. I seriously doubted that he had done a thing to it, that he had somehow misplaced the engine and that his months of excuses were intended to cover up the loss.

"It doesn't even look like my engine," I told Dunn.

"That isn't the same carburetor that was on there," Dunn said. "I had to go through a warehouse I know of and find a carburetor. But it's your engine, all right, rebuilt right down to the guts."

Jennifer and Andy were in the garage, scuffing the floor, looking at the ceiling. They sensed my frustration, knew by my silence that Dunn had somehow managed, however unintentionally, to ruin the project. He showed up with an engine two weeks before the show, an engine that I seriously doubted would start. Maybe I should have heeded Bud's warning. I could hear him in my head, saying, "I'd be worried about that engine if I were you."

I had called a towing service when Dunn pulled up in my alley. It took nearly an hour for the towing rig to arrive, an awkward hour in which it was hard to make conversation with Dunn. He was hanging around sheepishly, hoping to get some money, I suppose. When the tow truck arrived we rolled the boat from the garage into the alley. The tow truck driver winched the engine out of Dunn's trailer and then slowly lowered it onto the stringers in the boat, Dunn and I guiding the engine. I only hand-tightened the four big lug bolts that held the engine to the stringers, and then the tow truck driver and Dunn helped me push the boat back into the garage. The act of lifting the tongue of the trailer to push the boat tilted the boat enough that engine oil leaked out of the transmission seal at the back of the motor. I didn't notice it until the next day.

After I settled with the tow truck driver, I still had Dunn to deal with. He wanted money. I wouldn't pay him. What should have been one of the turning points of the project, one of the days of celebration, had turned sour. I told him as much, and he protested that he had, in fact, rebuilt the engine.

"How in the hell am I supposed to know that?" I said.

Dunn launched into a rambling soliloquy about the problems he had encountered making new bearings. Something wasn't right about his lonely discourse; he didn't seem to grasp the point that he had delivered to me an engine that by all accounts looked like scrap iron, a junk heap. Dunn said he'd return the next day to get it running, and I told him I expected as much because there wouldn't be any money until it ran.

Finally, Dunn left. I felt a twinge of something for him because he obviously wasn't the same man who had been recommended to me. Dozens of my calls to him had gone unreturned in the days before he finally showed up. When I did reach his home, his family either never knew where he was or pretended not to. Toward the end, they had taken to hanging up on me. After Pete Dunn drove away I knew he wasn't coming back.

"I went straight into the house and called you," I told Harry. "I would have gladly had you do the engine, but I remembered what you told me about not wanting to do any work for anybody, so I never bothered to get hold of you in the first place."

"I don't like going to somebody's house to tune up a motor," Harry said, making sure I understood the distinction. "You got it wrong. What I like to do is rebuild them."

"Wonderful," I said, "now you tell me."

The first time I ever saw Harry crouched in a bilge was at my father's house. I don't remember how I had ever gotten wind of Harry, but he had come over to perform precisely the chore he evidently had grown to dislike—tuning up a motor. It was the fall of 1982 and he had agreed to come over to attempt to start the Billy Joe House Sportsman. It hadn't been started in five years. Using a battery he brought with him, a remote starter switch, and a can of ether, Harry started it. It coughed and spit black exhaust sludge spots against the white garage door, but it ran and made a satisfying roar before he shut it down and claimed it to be reasonably fit for having been still for five years and fished out of the water before that.

"I was on the phone to you, Harry," I said, "before Pete Dunn ever cleared my alley."

Harry listened to all of it and then he said, "When's the show?"

"Two weeks," I said, "from yesterday."

"Ah, hell," Harry said, "that's plenty of time. You want another beer?"

14 〰〰〰〰〰〰〰〰〰〰〰〰

THE FIRST NIGHT AT HARRY'S was warm and starlit and noisy with crickets, out there where dew begins on the leading edge of suburban summer darkness. Harry lives on high ground, above the streamers of fog that sometimes floated in the hollows around him, in pockets of cooler air. The dirt street he fronted dead-ended just down the hill from his place where a few ranch-style houses were built on a cul-de-sac at the edge of a corn field.

From his open garage doors, looking south, White Bear Lake was the just-perceptible dip in the yonder tree line around the north shore of the lake, the feeling, looking out that way, that there was a lake down the road. Harry insisted that he didn't live far enough out, that if he moved again, it would be deeper into the country, to the north, near a lake called Big Marine; Harry insisted that the sheriff's water patrols on lakes that he loosely construed to be inside the metropolitan area were too harsh on boaters like Harry, who just wanted to loll about and drink beer while adrift. Moving to Big Marine would settle such a problem, getting him out of the reach of such unreasonable law enforcement.

When I drove up into the dirt-and-gravel driveway that first night, I heard music from an oldies station, the nasal harmonies and twangs of the late 1950s and early 1960s, the Sherry Baby stuff, the Four Seasons, Gene Chandler, early Beatles. Harry's pals were drinking beer and leaning on the boat, their pointy elbows stuck out like wings. Harry had taken the precaution of draping an old fuzzy blanket over the covering board the way a mechanic covers the fender of a car. As I walked up to the garage I could see Harry's bushy head of black hair inside the boat. He was crouched in the bilge, wrestling with the flywheel.

I said hello and was greeted silently, with a nod, one of them saying, "The guy is here, Harry."

"What did this Dunn do?" Harry said. He was talking to me while he looked at the engine.

I took my place alongside the boat.

"There isn't anything Harry can't fix," the guy next to me said. He was Harry's neighbor, a leathery, angular fellow with a slim, two-finger hold on the long amber neck of a Schmidt bottle. He was smoking a Lucky Strike straight. The pack was rolled up in the sleeve of his white T-shirt, the targetlike emblem on the cigarette pack visible through the thin cotton.

"You did a pretty job on this boat," the neighbor said.

A guy named Smoggy was in the boat with Harry. I never did learn his given name. He was a tough, fireplug of a guy, who evidently had a deviated septum, maybe from a fight in a hockey game, maybe from a fight in a bar. He said he played hockey. He could handle himself, I'd bet. Smoggy made clicking noises when he talked. Harry's brother, Randy, was there. Randy was slimmer than Harry, but their voices were so similar that you had to look at them to be sure which one was talking. They had a guy there named Teat, too. Teat had a big, friendly grin that showed perfect teeth. There was a smell I hadn't smelled in twenty years, on Teat, the Jade East cologne smell, a high-school-mixer smell.

"I don't know, Harry," I said, trying to sound as if I fit in. "You want to know what Dunn did? What he didn't do is more like it."

The flywheel wouldn't turn. The previous night, after I left for town and home, Harry had moved the boat into his garage, in the manner of taking in a guest. He had moved his fishing rig to the backyard to make room in the garage for my boat. He crawled around in the Chris Craft, he told me now, and determined that something was drastically wrong with the flywheel. Stiffness was permissible; the engine presumably had been rebuilt as contracted. But the flywheel was frozen. Harry, with arms as big as barrels, couldn't turn the wheel with a pry bar. I had walked in on the plan they had most recently agreed upon. They were attempting to turn the flywheel over with two batteries, the six-volt run through one of Harry's twelve-volts.

Harry rigged a remote wire and starter button to the starter on the side of the engine block, hooked up battery cables to the engine starter and engine block, and then tried to fire the engine over by depressing the remote starter button. The starter made an anemic, powerless whirring. The starter's strong steel teeth didn't spring out to catch on the matching teeth on the flywheel.

"Got to take the starter off," Smoggy said.

"Test it?" Harry said.

"Test it," Randy said.

Neighbor took a pull from the Schmidt bottle. Teat poked his head in there and looked as confused as I was.

"What's the matter, Harry?" I said.

"Aw, this Dunn guy screwed something up," Harry said. "Get in here."

I climbed into the boat.

"Can't believe it," Randy said. "A guy does a job like this on the boat, and the guy who does the engine screws everything up."

Harry put me to work. He told me what to unbolt and I did my damnedest. I barked every knuckle inside a minute's time. Harry took a beer break and lit a cigarette from the pack of Marlboro Lights he kept on the stern deck of his own fiberglass speedboat, the Rinker, a twenty-footer, with the 260 horsepower, 350 cubic-inch stern-driven MerCruiser. It was parked diagonally across two of the three garage stalls. The Rinker had a teak platform on the stern, for hoisting into the boat after swimming. Over my shoulder I was answering questions about the boat while also trying to give the impression that I knew how to unbolt a starter. Harry might as well have told me to design a nuclear reactor. I noticed that Harry had made progress with the wiring, that color-coded wires were bolted to terminals on the starter, and that the brass oil pressure tube was snugged onto its sending unit. It was starting to look like an operable engine.

Harry, a tool and die maker by trade with his own company, Woodland Tool, on Highway 61, was the son of a power company meterman. There were eight Zemke kids, Harry in the middle of the brood, none of whom ever strayed too far from White Bear.

They lived close to the lake, but across Highway 61, on the west side of it, when Harry was a boy. They had a lake easement at the foot of Seventh Street, where they kept their dock. Harry keeps a postcard in his cluttered office that shows a fantail rowboat, his father's boat, pulled up on the sand, Manitou Island and the Manitou Island Bridge in the background, a generic drugstore postcard. The photographer, back in the halcyon 1950s, just happened to catch the Zemke shoreline, so that postcards of the Zemke rowboat might be hanging on walls in New Zealand for all Harry knows.

We got to talking in the garage about the boats we remembered, boats that we hadn't paid that much attention to when we were younger.

"I remember my first ride in one of these buggers," Harry was saying. "I used to hang around the dock there at the boat works. I remember walking around in the shadows under those canvas Quonset hut covers, the smell under there of the water and the gasoline in the boats. Buster worked on the engines. He didn't have anybody helping him. One day he asked me to go for a ride with him and drive while he tinkered with the timing on one of them. I jumped in that boat, boy. I loved the sound that boat made."

"Remember that pump at Johnson's?" I said.

Harry started laughing. Then he took a big swallow of beer and belched, thus duplicating the sound of the pump. That pump is there to this day, though seldom used. In the heyday of the 1940s and 1950s, the Chris Crafts and Gar Woods and Centuries launched in the spring would soak in the rampway at the dock and then get pumped out by an apparatus that made the sounds of human agony, a sucking and gurgling sound. And to this day, my brother Johnny can duplicate that sound to perfection and is likely to do so at the most curious moments—in the middle of a Thanksgiving dinner, or stepping into sunlight after church.

"Remember Galloway's boat?" I said.

"Galloway doesn't ring a bell," Harry said.

"They kept it in a slip dredged out of the shoreline

at the foot of the peninsula," I told them. "A lagoon. There used to be a lagoon where I grew up, too, you can still see traces of it in the grass over there."

There were big trees around the Galloway slip, or lagoon. It was always dark and shady and cool in there, a wood framework supporting a tin roof over the lagoon. The boat was long and sleek and looked dark in the shadows of the slip. I remember that it had two flat, folding windshields and—here's the best part, I told Harry—a twelve-cylinder Wright Patterson airplane engine.

"No!" Harry said.

"When Galloway started that thing," I said, "our dock shook. We're across the lake and the dock shook."

I told him that I remembered that boat, a fleeting picture of it passing by with its enormous air ventilators and chrome horns and lights, flying its pennants. My father remembered it as a Johnson-built boat, although he allowed that it could have been a Hacker Craft. It was fashioned more along the lines of a grand old Hacker than of any other make.

Harry's first resurrection, he said, was the 1951 Chris Craft Riviera. The engine was missing when he found the hull in White Bear township. His detective work led him back to one of the boat's previous owners, just down the shore from where I grew up. He was told that the engine was buried on the beach. Harry dug it up and rebuilt it. The parts he needed for it—even bolts—he made himself.

Randy once had a Century. Doing it in reverse of the way I had done it, Harry and Randy had brilliantly restored their boats to mechanical perfection while only begrudgingly taking care of the hulls. Randy's boat, for example, flying across the lake at about forty miles per hour two minutes after he had launched it for the first time in fifteen years, began to sink. Harry, chasing him in the fishing boat, motioned for him to head for shore. In knee-deep water, Randy's boat nestled to the bottom.

"I didn't caulk it," Randy said. "You could see right through the cracks in the bottom, but I thought she'd swell up."

"Well, they do swell," I said, "but it takes days."

"I was anxious to try the engine," Randy said.

They started howling and clicking and belching and farting, the ones who knew him best calling Randy a dumb shit, but in such ritualistic, lodgelike fashion that it seemed natural. I liked the sudden feeling of being with company, with others, with the like-minded. Years ago, in high school, I had owned a Model A Ford. I tinkered with it endlessly, and when my buddies would come over and ask me to go somewhere, I would beg off to devote myself to the mysteries of the Ford, and I'd say to them, "Half the fun's working on it."

Harry's crowd would have known what I meant. They were deeply and incontrovertibly devoted to the internal combustion engine. They were in love with motors. Life in the summer revolved round the garage and Schmidt beer. When the beer supply ran out Harry would fish into his cutoff jeans for a ten- or twenty-dollar bill and holler for Linda. Linda would gather up her two girls and the wives and girlfriends of the garage occupants and go sailing off for beer, her hair flying, driving Harry's 1968 Ford convertible.

"I got it!" I said. The starter came off heavy in my hands, a piece of equipment about as big as a football. I passed it out of the boat, and Harry set it down on the garage floor. It didn't test out strong.

"Dunn never checked this out," Harry said. "I'm

afraid you'll be doing a lot of work on things that this Dunn never checked out."

A wave of panic swept over me, the ticking clock. The show was thirteen days and counting.

"You take the starter with you tonight," Harry said, "and tomorrow morning you go to G & R Rebuilding on Prior near University. You know where that is? You go in there and tell them you suspect a bad field. They'll know what to do and they'll do it quick. Tell them it's a rush job."

"Bad field?"

"Bad electrical field," Harry said.

"G & R," I said, "Prior and University. I got that. What if they can get it done tomorrow?"

"Then bring it out tomorrow night," Harry said. "There's no more we can do right now."

I stayed long enough to drink another Schmidt. I hated Schmidt beer, but I didn't know Harry well enough yet to risk offending him.

15 $\wedge\wedge\wedge\wedge\wedge\wedge\wedge\wedge\wedge\wedge\wedge\wedge\wedge\wedge$

IT WAS FLUKY THAT I HAD FOUND HARRY at home on the weekend that Pete Dunn had left me high and dry and panicked in my own garage, in my own alley, counting days until the show. After the first week out at Harry's place, after having raced out there every night, the feverish work bringing the show closer to reality, Harry announced that he and his family were going away for the weekend, towing the Rinker up to Big Sandy, a lake in northern Minnesota where Harry had a sliver of shoreline property. That left me one week to go before the show and still a load of work to do on the engine.

"Harry, come on, I'm worried here," I said on the Thursday of my first week with him. He was leaving the next day.

The rebuilt starter, incidentally, didn't spin the flywheel, but it wasn't the starter's fault after all. The flywheel was binding on the engine castings. In addition, two of the four flywheel bolt studs were stripped. Harry was astonished at the mess he had been begged into cleaning up. Harry removed the flywheel and took it to his Woodland Tool, a pale yellow building about the size of a three-car garage. As delicately as a dentist working on a tooth, Harry machined thousandths of an inch off the heavy flywheel. We had the engine freely spinning by the time Harry left for Big Sandy. We had some of the electrical components rebuilt. We were getting closer.

"But, Harry, there's only a week left before the show."

"You can work over the weekend in my garage," Harry said, "or you can haul the boat over to your folks, whatever. Change the transmission seal, that's what you could do over the weekend, change that thing and it's one less job we got next week."

"Explain this seal thing to me one more time," I said.

We were in Harry's garage. Darkness was chasing dusk. It was hot. Jesus H. I did not want Harry to leave for an entire weekend. I wanted to get the boat done. I didn't trust myself to change the seal—for God's sake, a seal. I might have exaggerated by saying that unbolting a starter was like asking me to design a nuclear reactor, but a seal genuinely terrified me. It was like that sinking feeling you get when an automobile mechanic discovers a "rear seal" is leaking. You imagine the axle will have to be dropped from its moorings and special tools and the precision of a heart surgeon will be required for going deep inside things.

I felt in trouble, abandoned.

I towed the boat away from Harry's place on Friday afternoon and drove halfway around the lake to the east shore, to my parents' house at Mahtomedi, not more than five miles from Harry's. I flew a piece of orange cloth from the newly chromed stern lifting ring, my warning to the world to please brake; the trailer still had no brake lights. I backed the boat into the garage at my parents', in the same third stall where we had kept the Billy Joe House Sportsman all those years.

It was a warm night. The lake was glistening, oily-looking in the golden moments when the sun begins its descent. The east shore is the most interesting on a lake, I am convinced, the quietness of the morning with the sun coming up behind you, the sometimes near-violence of the north and west winds that rattle the lakefront windows, an east wind usually modest after all and bringing only rain or a change of weather, the exquisite sunsets in the summer, the icy snowscape in the winter when the lake looks like the moon and the sky burns red in the dead of a January dusk.

I could hear the voices of swimmers at the beach next door, on the other side of what we called the swamp. I made a note to go in there with a shovel someday and root around for Liedl's old Chris Craft windshield brackets, find them, clean them, and probably get a few hundred dollars for them at one of the boat club swap meets.

It had been a calm day, not much wind at all. That's why the stirred-up lake looked oily and glistening. A wind would have skimmed the water, making it look fresh. Bud hobbled out of the house and grew irritated at having to leave a car out overnight, as though he had to leave one on the street. The driveway was Y-shaped, entrances off the street on either side of the garage and then a straight portion of the driveway, the stem of the Y, running up to the house. His irritation was faked; there was room for a dozen cars in the driveway.

"Three nights at the most," I said, "tonight, tomorrow, and Sunday and then back to Harry's. He went to Big Sandy for the weekend."

"What are you going to do?" he said. He was just

two weeks or so out of the hospital. His arm was in a sling.

"Change the transmission seal," I said.

He made a wincing face that suggested he was sorry that he had asked.

"You'll need a gear puller," he said.

Harry had cautioned me to get a gear puller. The seal itself was an eighty-cent piece of material, a metal ring with a rubber ring inside the metal, about as big around as the top to a peanut butter jar. It was getting to its location at the back of the engine that was tricky.

Bud and I talked about it out in the duskiness of the garage, Bud having produced a padded card-table chair to sit on. His was a big, handsome three-stall garage, one of my favorites, as garages go. I had another boat up against the back wall of it, a 1951 seventeen-foot Chris Craft special runabout, a White Bear boat that I picked up in the fall of 1984 for a song, a boat I would get to someday, but not any time soon, not while the utility was so close to the top of the charts. In the rafters of the garage there were pieces still from the Billy Joe House Sportsman, an old floor-model radio up there, too, water skis, an ancient adult-sized tricycle that my younger brothers and sisters dusted off for neighborhood parades. On the Fourth of July, and on the holidays that bracketed the summer months, Labor and Memorial Days, they laced the spokes of the ancient three-wheeler with crepe paper and streamers.

"The boat looks beautiful," Bud said. Without knowing precisely when in the last decade, I had come to love these moments when he watched me tinker with boats, in my garage or his.

"We never had the utility in here, did we?" I said, meaning the one that got away to settle the account at Johnson's.

"Always stored at Johnson's," he said.

"But you kept the Sportsman here," I said, meaning The Boat That Broke Loose from the Car.

"We kept that one alongside the garage," he said, "covered with a big tarp."

His sling clamped his arm pathetically close to his chest, like a wounded wing. He did not look right having to tolerate a sling or the long weeping gash where infection had set in after the surgery to restore movement to his fingers. Those fingers, scarcely able to be wiggled, would never recover, the whole hand a thick, raw clump of flesh now. He was once a great squash player, but more to the example of dexterity, he was once a great bicycle repairman. At regular intervals during summer months he sat out on the garage on an overturned galvanized pail, approximately where he was sitting now, and adjusted the bicycles brought to his attention, one after the other.

Now he looked old in the half-light of the garage, the light playing cruelly on his jowls in a way that made them look heavy, giving his face a drooping look, not like him at all. If I had tried to reconcile myself to his inevitable death, the other endings in his life were still just as painful to us both. The end of his working career. The end of most of his associations. Even the big house where my brothers and sisters and I were raised was sure enough coming to an end, the ending of an entire century on that piece of land on the lake that we loved. The house was too big for two people, too demanding, too expensive, too noisy with its silences of departed children, none of whom had struck it big enough to relieve our father of the financial burden of keeping the place going.

I would miss that place, miss it terribly. So would he. I couldn't get him to say it, but I just knew he would miss it because sometimes I caught him staring out at the water and I bet he could see a long way back into his own time there, his own sweet, holy, and haunting history. Paul told me of a scene that I wish I had been there to see and hear. Bud was looking out at the lake, the sun suspended above the west shore of the lake, the fiery ball of orange power that had hung there like that every night since the beginning of time.

"It's never dropped," Bud said of the sun. "I've been watching that sun for seventy years and it's never dropped."

For some reason, when Paul told me about it I wondered if it was a fear Bud had had as a child, he and his brother Phil, that maybe the sun would fall into the water with a boiling hiss. Or, more likely, that Bud sensed his own mortality, the extraordinary marshaling of his energies that was needed to live out his life's plan reminding him of the strength it took for the sun to hang in the sky.

"So there's nothing I can do tonight," I said. "Maybe go for a swim and then head back to town. I have the seal, but I'll have to rent a gear puller tomorrow and do this thing. I can rent one from that rent-all place in White Bear near Tousley."

I mentioned a Ford dealer across the lake, with a rental place located across the street.

"Or Al's," Bud said, talking about Al Hardy's service station, just up the hill and back off the main village road, next to Vince Guarnera's place, Vince selling real estate and insurance these days. "Al might have a puller you could use. See what happens."

We all drove out the next day, a sunny Saturday. Jennifer, Andy, Emily, and the baby went swimming. I installed myself in the garage. The sun was baking the shingled roof of the garage and heating up the insides. Al Hardy had loaned me a gear puller, sure enough, and I conned

Paul into giving me a hand. It was going to be one of those days, the sweat stinging our eyes before we even got settled to the task.

We unbolted the shaft from the back of the motor. We also backed off the two rear engine mount lug bolts, so that the motor could be lifted slightly. The seal fit into the transmission at the back of the motor, after we first extracted, with a gear puller, the hub, or flange. The shaft had been bolted to the hub. Once exposed, the old seal could be picked out after first spinning off a nut approximately the size of a hockey puck. Luckily, Harry had given me a homemade socket that fit the nut and his ratchet driver to accommodate it.

"So tell me," Paul said, as we sat crouched in the bilge with the sweat burning our eyes and running down our faces, "what in the hell are you doing?"

"I'm taking this nut off here," I said, meaning the one the size of the puck.

But first, holding the nut in place was a washer with tabs. The tabs had to be pried out of the nut's reverse path with a screwdriver. I succeeded. Paul supplied the leverage that raised the back of the engine just high enough for me to wield the various tools. Paul used a pry bar, lodging the end of it on a chunk of wood placed on the bottom of the boat and then slowly exerting enough pressure that the motor rose ever so slightly off its rear mounts, thus making the transmission accessible.

The seal to be replaced evidently was so worn, or worn away, that when Dunn had at last filled the engine with new oil, the oil ran directly past the seal and out into the bilge the moment the boat was slightly tilted to favor the stern. As I looked at it, I suddenly understood that the seal rode back and forth on the apparatus that determined forward and reverse gearing. I plucked out the old seal—it was definitely deteriorated—and set in place the new.

"Learn something new every day, boy," I said.

Paul was a junior in college, but he had been boy to the rest of us from his day one. He was five years old in my wedding pictures and had given us a wedding present, a cartoon drawing of the lake, Johnson's visible across the lake, a lean-to, with stick men standing in front of it. Our relationship was virtually nonexistent until the discovery of the Billy Joe House Sportsman, when I was just shy of thirty and Paul was eleven. I am my father's son at that, conveniently enough having a boat handy in order to reintroduce myself to my brother. By July 1986, Paul's fascination with old boats had long since worn off. We easily enough met on other, more common grounds: golf, hockey, sailing in all its forms, even conversation for its own sake, which, I believe, sometimes surprised both of us.

Bud found us just as we had finished with the seal. He was drinking a beer. Andy arrived moments later, with a towel around his narrow shoulders, leaving wet footprints on the warm concrete floor. Despite the heat in the garage, Andy was shivering.

"Andy," his grandfather told him. "It's hot in here."

Andy stopped shivering long enough to consider the information.

"Papa," he said, "you're right."

16 〰〰〰〰〰〰〰〰〰〰〰

"HEY, HARRY," I SAID, walking in on him in his garage.

"What?" Harry's voice came from the bilge of the boat, the voice a littled muffled.

"I hate Schmidt beer," I said.

The plastic cooler was on the floor next to the boat, bottles of Schmidt on ice.

"Naw, Joe," Harry said, speaking into the motor, "you got to love the Schmidt."

"I'm telling you, Harry," I said, "I'm bringing out some Old Style, some Miller, anything. Leinenkugel's. You ever drink Leinenkugel's?"

"I don't drink beer I can't spell," Harry said.

"Beer should have a taste to it, Harry," I said. "I read someplace it should have a little apple flavoring. That's how you know it's good, it tastes like apples, I guess."

"I want it to taste like beer, like Schmidt," Harry said, "Ummmm, I love that Schmidt."

"Harry, you drink this in the winter?"

"Love that Schmidt in the winter," Harry said,

straightening up, his bones creaking from the crouch in the bilge. "Only difference in the winter, we got snowmobiles in here instead of boats."

"Harry, you're crazy."

"Probably," Harry said.

I was glad and relieved to have the boat back in Harry's garage. I took the week off from work, the final week before the show, the big push. We gathered every night— Harry, Randy, Smoggy, sometimes the neighbor. Teat came and went. I figured that by now I knew Harry well enough to insult his beer. He took it well. We were getting to know each other, the boat providing a convenient excuse to reminisce about the shared themes of our lives, a life on the water, around it, near it, winter and summer, the pull of the water.

The starter, generator, voltage regulator, fuel pump, carburetor, coil, and spark plug wires had to be either rebuilt or replaced. Virtually everything had to be rebuilt in record time, so there began a frantic shuttling to town and back with all the parts that should have been fixed by the Dunner. That's what we came to call Dunn: the Dunner. In our sometimes desperate, slap-happy state, with the nighttime gnats buzzing around our ears and the beer making us sweat like chain gang convicts, we played silly etymological games until Dunn finally acquired his new name.

"Jesus Christ," Harry kept saying, "what did this Dunner do, find engine parts on the side of the road and then stick them together?"

My education, though not total, was revealing. I made it to the back rooms of most of the small part rebuilding shops in town, the rooms where the wooden floors are oil-stained and worn out from weary foot traffic, the rooms with the 1964 calendar still on the wall, the shot of the bare-breasted girl looking back over her pale shoulder, the rooms where men in overalls pick at the insides of their ears with stubs of pencil, the rooms that smell of electrical friction and graphite and thin lubricating oil, the kind of places where you can still, in the home stretch of the twentieth century, get a generator tested out on a work-bench blackened with oil and cluttered with ancient and discarded pieces of iron and spring and coil.

I came to know Joe and Mike and Larry and Wayne, each of them reminiscent of old Buster, who was not so old when I was a boy. Buster, the mechanical arm of the Johnson brothers at the boat works across the lake, had his own machine shop just to the right as you entered the boat works through tall, sea-green doors. Buster's place was cool and shadowed; a workbench ran along the length of the wall under darker-green-tinted windows that looked out into the yard between the main boat works and one of the stor-age sheds. Amidst the tall grass and piles of lumber in the yard was a Model A Ford panel truck, backed up to an opening in the wall, behind which was a tin chute. Three or four times a year, Buster's crew shoveled the sweepings and the trimmings down the chute, and the truck labored away to the dump with its sweet-smelling cargo of sawdust and cedar scrap.

The old shops I visited reminded me of Johnson's, of the way Johnson's held a singularly important status in our lives because things happened there, things got fixed there. Going to Johnson's on Saturdays with my father to get gas for the old utility always began as an adventure.

From my father's perspective, incidentally, getting gas was just an errand. It was an adventure only to me, a spe-cial Saturday adventure in which I was given duties to per-form that taken together, conspired to make me an almost equal partner in the adult action. For starters, I would install the drain plug down in the bilge. Then cautiously, turning my head away from the ominous cables, I'd help to lower the boat from the weathered timbers that supported the ancient cable and winch mechanism, the cable slivery to the accidental touch. With boat floating, straining gently against the cable hooks still in the lifting rings, my father would choke it and work the starter button. I'd hang my head over the rear deck, anticipating the first spit of water through the nub of copper exhaust pipe in the transom.

"A-OK," I'd report to him at the wheel. I'd hop to the front deck and free the hook, then scurry to the rear and do the same, hanging the hooks back up out of the way on the U of the big pulleys bolted to the cross-timbers of the hoist. We'd be off, still moving about, though, like conscientious deckhands. There was still the stern flag to unfurl. So insistent was my father on a freely flying flag that to this day I notice if flags are wrapped once, twice, three times around their poles and staffs, and not just on boats, but in front of government buildings and schools.

Finally, I'd take my place beside him; he'd be hatless, wearing a white shirt rolled up to his elbows. The boat works was so directly across the lake from our place that on calm mornings its distorted shape seemed to lean out across the lake like an image in a funhouse mirror, like the wedding present picture of it that my brother drew with crayons. The sun played the same optical trick on the White Bear water tower and on the cars that looked as fat and slow-moving as beetles along Clark Street and Highway 61. On the flat mornings we'd lower the windshield, advance the throttle, and try to get the beast to plane. Under way, making our own breeze, the smell of the bilge was potent, exclusively of gas and oil, this being an active boat with an active bilge, a bilge not yet gone to seed.

Sometimes Buster—his real name was Walter—appeared in the big doorway and hobbled down to the dock when he saw us pull in. He was arthritic, probably from crawling around in boats, banging his shins and knees. Buster always wore khaki. His silver hair was brushed back in a flattop. Although he was an extraordinarily gentle man with almost a quiver in his voice, Buster had the full tough face of a prizefighter, like a Dead End kid in his fifties.

Buster was engines. His brother Iver was sailboats. There was a Milton, too, known as Pete. Pete wore dark-green work suits. He was a big man, with thin wisps of black hair that drooped down over his forehead. He wore glasses. I don't recall that he worked on sailboats. On the rare occasion when he worked on an engine he'd wrestle with it for a spell and then say, "Ah, let Buster do it."

"Remember Pete?" I asked my father once. "If Iver was sailboats and Buster was engines, what was Pete in charge of?"

"Food," my father said.

During the gassing ritual, I'd wander up from the dock and enter the coolness of the place and smell the glue and the cedar used in the construction of the sailboats. Spilled glue stained the wooden floors in dark clumps, like spilled molasses. The sailboats were on jigs, with unused jigs in the rafters. Sawdust was thick on the floors, as thick as the smell of varnish in the air. Off the main workroom was a high-ceilinged storage barn, with sailboats on slings above the three-pointed motorboats; in the winter the motorboats were put in there every which way, a bow here, a stern there, no rhyme or reason for the pattern, except that everything fit and ended up with a roof over it.

Buster's mechanical wing was a foreign place to me then. It was dark, with dozens of batteries on the floor and engines suspended on chain hoists from tracks in the ceiling. Buster machined the hardware for the sailboats, too, so that there were boxes of cleats and pulleys and wooden spools of cable for the mast stays—all of this plus that Rockwell-like view he had out the green-tinted outward opening windows, of the yard, the tall yellow grasses, the Model A truck, the storage barn yonder and under the storage barn, slots, with sailboats stored three deep in each one in the winter, slots empty and grass-grown in the summer.

There were offices, too, Iver always in charge in the office, beautiful photographs on the walls of sailboats heeling over, of the children of Iver and Buster sailing the boats and smiling at the spray flying over their yellow slickers. There was a photo as well of John O., the man who started it all, and his grandson, Paul, Iver's boy. Paul was seated on John O.'s angled drawing table, John O. making a model scow, bits of wire and wood and a scissors on his drawing table.

By the time I got back to the dock, my father would be signing the gas bill and leaving the receipt in a metal box with a hinged lid on the top of the gas tank. It was for a summer's worth of those bills that he had turned the boat over to Johnson's.

About a third of the way back home we'd stop and throw the boat in reverse to clear weeds from the prop. Looking back at the shore, the sun higher now, our eyes no longer played optical tricks, and it looked to be a normal place, the cars no longer looking like bugs. My father would have me drive and he'd sit in the back seat, pretending to be chauffeured.

There were philosophical descendants of Buster in all those shops I stormed, a labor force of men who had not been lured away by the promise of money into law or computer science or consulting work. I had electrical fields explained to me, and gears and gaskets. And each summer night, with something new repaired, the engine a little closer to spark and life, I'd rush back to Harry's. It came down to the final task on Tuesday, August 5, four days before the show: we intended to run the engine in Harry's driveway, with a garden hose supplying water to the engine block.

It was about 8 P.M. when five of us rolled the boat out of Harry's garage. It was warm and humid. The gnats were thick. A haze settled over the rural fields that rolled off in the distance from Harry's side yard. The neighbor said, "Don't worry, Harry can fix anything." Harry crouched in the bilge and waited as the water from the garden hose ran its course through the block and the jackets and finally into a trickle expelled from the exhaust pipe. The trickle of water indicated to Harry that the Dunner had not boiled out the block as he more properly might have.

"Mice," Harry said.

Smoggy, Teat, Randy, and the neighbor nodded their assent.

"Mice?" I said, pacing up and down alongside the boat, "what do you mean, mice?"

"Field mice make nests in the engine," Harry said. "It's no big deal."

Harry sprayed ether into the flame arrester on the carburetor and hand-choked it as long as he was down there. He worked in a catcher's crouch, a spare tire of Schmidt beer hanging over his belt in a liquid jiggle. His T-shirt was darkly stained with sweat. Randy, standing even with the steering wheel, reached in from outside the boat and ran the throttle and starter button. Smoggy was on the other side of the boat, ready to single-handedly hold it back, I guess, if it took off.

Unlike Bud's utility, mine had a fancier toggle-switch

ignition, like that of a Model A Ford. Bud's had a key and starter button. When I had my instruments rebuilt, the rebuilder soldered over the keyhole—the tumbler had disintegrated—and wrote back with instructions to either rig up a new key ignition or just use the switch in its on position, with the starter button hot-wired to the switch. I chose the second option. Harry wired it so that you turned the switch lever to on and pressed the button.

"Do it," Harry said.

Randy hit the button, and the engine spun and coughed once. Harry dusted the carb again with ether. "Do it again." This time it caught and made a roar to bring the house down, a roar that echoed out over the countryside.

I did a little war dance of whooping and hollering, raising my fist in the air. Harry, watching me, smiled like a big cat as he worked down close to the roar, adjusting the carburetor jets with a screwdriver.

Harry touched the block, thought it too hot, and then made a cut sign across his throat. Randy turned the switch to the off position. The silence was full of aftershock. My ears rang.

"It's not getting enough water," Smoggy said.

We waited until the block had cooled and started it again. Randy revved it this time, and bits of nest and debris blew out the exhaust, indicating that the water jackets were opening up. It ran cooler then, and we let it run at high speed for about three minutes—it seemed like an hour while I cowered from the explosion I certainly anticipated—and then brought it down to the low speed idle so that the water burbled out the stern and it made the noise we all had been waiting for, the bup, bup, bup, bup, gurgle, bup, bup, bup, gurgle.

I war-danced again.

Harry said, "Sounds good."

Satisfied, Harry gave Randy a second cut sign. In the sudden silence water dripped from the exhaust and settled onto the clay driveway, making a stream that ran into the street in front of Harry's and down the hill. Harry disconnected the garden hose apparatus, gathered up his tools, and climbed out of the boat.

"Only one thing left," Harry said. "Let's water-test it tomorrow."

We had no sooner agreed that I would come out early and tow the boat to the launching ramp at the foot of Manitou Island than two headlight beams turned into Harry's street and then into the driveway. It was Bud, my mother taking him around.

"Damn!" I said. "You just missed it. We had it running."

"No!" he said, bending to the task of walking up the slight grade with the help of his cane.

The headlights of his car illuminated the boat's lingering exhaust. The smell of ether was still in the air. He limped up for a look, his arm in the sling. My mother got out and folded her arms across her chest, watching where she was walking to avoid the trail of muddy water.

"Did it explode?" she said.

Harry said he had everything under control. He called his elders Mr. and Mrs.

"You going to make the show?" Bud said.

"He should make it," Harry said. "We'll water-test it tomorrow."

I planned to keep the boat on a hoist at the dock next to my family's house. The hoist was vacant, and I already had asked permission. I wanted it to sit low on the hoist for at least twenty-four hours so the bottom would swell—twenty-four hours wasn't enough time for a proper swelling, but it was all I had.

"We're launching it tomorrow morning," I said. "You'll hear us coming. Damn, I wish you could have heard it tonight, though. It really sounded good."

"I bet it did," Bud said.

17

WEDNESDAY, LAUNCH DAY, was perfect, a high, clear sky and eighty degrees by 10 A.M. The water at the launching ramp at the foot of Manitou Island was calm and gemstone green, but a flawed gemstone, a hint of dog days on the water. A slight breeze moved bluer water in gentle ripples just off the shore of the island, the same island that Mark Twain wrote about in *Life on the Mississippi*, in which he included the legend of the Indian warrior and the white bear, from which the lake takes its name.

A car leaving the island rattled the loose boards on the narrow wooden bridge connecting the island to the grove of public land called Matoska Park, where there was a gazebo and a small wooden bandshell. Two fishermen with cane poles were fishing over the railing of the bridge, bobbers floating in the shadows beneath them. The launching was silent, the kind of silence that occurs only on late summer weekdays when there is no hurry on a lake, no recreational boating traffic, and just a few fishermen puttering so quietly along that you can hear their oars banging aluminum and even their conversations when they are hundreds of yards offshore.

Algae floated like dust on the green water near shore. When the boat slid off the trailer, it made an outward pushing ring of the algae and then sat buoyantly in a pool of freshly cleared and darkened water. I should have had a bottle of champagne to crack over the cutwater. Instantly, the deeply varnished sides shimmered golden on the water. The corklike buoyancy impressed me most, startled me, took my breath. During the years of restoration, I would forget how neatly they float and tug at themselves in the water. In a landlocked city garage there was always the fear that all the work might literally go down the drain, that even with modern caulks and chemicals it would be impossible to overcome twenty-five years of neglect in a farmer's field.

When I got in it for the first time at the launching dock, it was tippy. I had to remind myself that when such a boat was in our family, I was a weed of a boy weighing maybe eighty or ninety pounds. Now it felt like a toy boat to me. What had been so unwieldy on land and on the trailer seemed light and maneuverable and eager to be under way.

It was a rite of passage years ago when Bud's utility was launched in the spring at Johnson's, a literal waiting for our ship to come in. The boats were fetched from storage, presumably systematically, and then backed down the ramp with the workhorse jeep nosing them into the water. Our boat was always dusty from its layup, a storage tag with our name scrawled on it in grease pencil wired to one of the lifting rings. In the spring there were days when the docks at Johnson's were crowded with launched boats, days when Buster had to take on another mechanic just to install batteries and get the tubs running.

"I think our boat's in," I remember my father saying

annually in the spring, our version of Opening Day. To Johnson's way of thinking, the boats might have been launched systematically, but there was no rhyme or reason to the schedule as far as the customers were concerned. In fact, the burden was on the customer to check the docks, and I remember more than once the pleasant feeling of surprise when our boat was at last spotted in the cove in front of the boat works. Arrangements were made—whether my mother would drive my father to Johnson's, then when, then how many children would be involved—all to get the boat back home and hanging under its timbers, ready for another summer.

Harry and Randy followed me down to the ramp from Harry's in Harry's black Bronco. Harry's fishing rig was hitched to the Bronco. After my boat was in and floating, Harry backed in his fishing boat. Randy, who surprised me by producing a video camera, intended to drive alongside Harry and me and run circles around us as we made our way a mile or so across the lake to my parents' house. In direct contradiction of the disheveled and carefree persona he hauls around, Harry is remarkably conscientious. He wanted to bring along an extra battery and urged me to have an extra battery on hand for the show.

The show was three days off.

The engine popped over at the launching dock and idled nicely. But we didn't leave. The water pump didn't draw water. We had bypassed the water pump the night before when we started it on land, running Harry's garden hose directly into the engine until the water circulated through the water jackets. That's what Harry had been feeling for when he had placed his hand on the head—the telltale coolness of circulating water.

Now we knew what we must have at least subconsciously feared. Like everything else that Dunn was supposed to have fixed, he evidently hadn't touched the water pump. We might as well have been on a desert without a canteen. The only thing that quickly occurred to me was to speed over to my parents' house and remove the water pump from the engine of the 1951 Chris Craft special runabout. The engine in the special was the 1951 version of the same Chris Craft Model K that was in the utility. The water pumps were interchangeable.

We had no option. Randy towed us to a dock 200 or so yards north of the launching ramp, both Randy and Harry reminiscing that they were very near to the dock of their boyhood. There was a small sailboat, a catamaran, on a hoist at the dock, and on the sandy beach was a screen house with latticework under the porch and a life ring roped to the decking around the porch. There were picnic tables on the shore, too, and then thick brush and trees that hid the beach from the road above.

Paul, who was aware of our launching schedule, finally hove into view on Bud's pontoon boat. We explained our problem to him, and he volunteered to stay with the utility until we returned with the water pump. Randy intended to sun himself on the dock, like a turtle.

Off we went in Harry's rig, the boat show clock suddenly chiming like Big Ben. We clipped along faster than I've ever gone in a fishing boat. Harry explained that he had rebuilt the old green-hooded Johnson twenty-five-horse engine on the back and juiced it up just a tad.

At my parents' house, my mother looked out from an upstairs window and my father from behind a screen door. I shouted the predicament to them as I ran under the willows between the house and the swamp.

"Gotta get a new water pump."

Harry was in no mood to run. He strolled along behind me, picking up the explanation where I left off. He found me in the garage in due time. I was crouched in the bilge of the special, unbolting the water pump, shaving skin off my knuckles, working in the yellow beam of a weak flashlight. I told Harry the story of the special, how, on a tip, I had found it outside a barn on the grounds of an estate in Gem Lake, a private enclave of exclusive homes between White Bear and St. Paul. I had paid $600 for the special.

Water pump in hand, I detoured through the house, found two cans of beer in the basement refrigerator, and shouted out, "We'll be back." I passed a beer to Harry and off we went, tearing across the calm water again.

Paul was in awe of the utility when we arrived. He'd spent forty-five minutes photographing it from every angle with his thirty-five millimeter. He was most impressed by its buoyancy, for he, too, was a veteran of our other principal launch effort, the dramatically leaking Billy Joe House Sportsman of three years earlier.

"I can't believe it," Paul said.

"I can't either," I said, meaning the difficulty.

I unbolted the bad water pump and bolted on the new one. Harry watched me. Randy stirred himself from his snooze on the dock and began videotaping. We started the engine again by noon, and the pump worked, a minor miracle. We made a flotilla, the pontoon boat on one side, then the utility, then Randy in the fishing boat. Harry wore a life preserver, in case, he said, he had to tumble over the side after a loose beer. We idled slowly while Harry ran his hand over the block, satisfied with its coolness. Only slowly did I advance the throttle.

The bow lifted and our wake stretched out white and green, with an oversplash of green spray. The point of the bow looked so close, another reminder of how small the boat seemed to me now that I was actually in it and under way at last. We ran along the calm, lee side of Manitou Island, the shoreline lush, the houses on the island looking cool and gracious behind the shutters and awnings.

We came around the end of the island into the main body of the lake, heading for the Mahtomedi home shore. Paul broke ahead, sending up the twin rooster tails of the pontoon, and Randy circled us, getting new angles on his videotape. I sat on the covering board, steering casually with one hand as though I had made the trip a thousand times. To my ear the engine sounded rough, but Harry advised me that it was new, that it needed breaking in.

"It sounds OK," he said, adding, "I think." I could scarcely hear him above the racket. When I had brought the boat to Harry's ten days before, I had left the engine cover, the doghouse, back home. The boat didn't have its seats in it yet, either, and the floor wasn't secured. The floorboards were soiled with our footprints.

As we cleared the point of the peninsula, I tried the horn. The deep metallic beep echoed under the front deck, where, if I bent my head down, I could feel the heat and smell the unmistakable fumes of nostalgia. Beep. I did it again. Up ahead I could see that Paul had landed the pontoon at our dock. He was running up through the yard, a small figure from this distance out.

Beep. Beep. Beep.

Closer, closer, until I had to throttle down for the approaching east shore. I saw my father come out of the side door of the house and limp through the dappled shade in the front yard, working his way to the dock. I made a pass in front of the dock and then another, waiting for him to reach the end of the dock.

"I did it!" I said, passing close and then swerving out again, showing off at slow speed, clasping my hands overhead like a prizefighter.

He sat on the end of the bench, grinning and turning his whole frame to watch the movement of the boat. My mother followed him down and waved as she walked to the end of the dock to join him. We came in then and parked across the front section of the dock. My mother spent her entire life waiting for boats to explode, and now was no different.

"Joe, that won't explode, will it?" she said.

"Not for at least another ten minutes," I told her.

"It doesn't sound right," my father said, ignoring the prospects of an explosion.

"How's that?" Harry said.

"Sounds like it's missing," my father said. "It's timed, isn't it?"

"Timed by ear," Harry said.

"Well, that's how we used to do it," Bud said.

"I just think it's stiff," Harry said. "Maybe I should listen from the dock. Joe, you take it out and do a fly by."

Harry got out, and the boat rose a foot in the water. Harry pushed me away, and I was alone in it for the first time. I took off down the shoreline. But when I tried to give it full throttle, it balked, coughed, and sputtered. It ran well at half speed. I brought it back to the dock.

"It's missing," Bud said.

Harry climbed back in, and we went out again. He turned the distributor with his hand, trying to time it by sound, but we could not get it to go to full speed. We were taking on a little water now, too, and there were dollops of oil floating on the water sloshing around in the bilge. I tried not to notice. The vibration of the engine probably opened up the seams a little, but it was nothing drastic.

I was under way at last, but I felt heavy with the load of final preparations. There were just seventy-two hours before the show.

18 〰〰〰〰〰〰〰

IT BECAME STUCK IN MY MIND that I needed to haul the boat to the show on a new trailer. Unfortunately, it was typical of my personality that I would introduce such a new burden to the project with forty-eight hours to go. Nevertheless, once stuck, my mind is a trap. After about 200 phone calls I found a suitable trailer at a boat dealer on the outskirts of St. Paul.

I didn't necessarily want to own a new trailer, mind you. I just wanted to rent one.

"But we don't rent," I was told at the boat dealer out on Robert Street.

"If I buy it," I said, "and it doesn't fit the boat just right, can I bring it back?"

"Yes, but you'll forfeit a one-hundred-dollar deposit."

"I will agree to that," I said.

Which is exactly what I did. I used the trailer for the weekend and returned it the Monday after the show, thus renting it for $100, an entirely reasonable fee for such a road-worthy trailer.

The trailer turned out to be the least of my problems in the final push before the show. Incredibly, I had to replace the transmission seal one more time. The globules of oil floating in the bilge water on launch day were a telltale sign of another broken seal, this time because the seal Paul and I had put in over the weekend was from old Minnetonka Boat Works stock and had broken apart after a few transmission shifts because of age; the seal had deteriorated on the stockroom shelf. I called Jennifer and asked her to pick up a seal from an auto parts dealer that Harry recommended. Jennifer did the running, bought the seal, and brought it out to White Bear. I had it installed by late afternoon of launch day, and then the whole gang of us, me, Harry, Harry's wife, their two girls, Jennifer, Andy, Emily, and the baby sat around in the front yard of Bud's place waiting for dusk to go dark over the lake, cooling out from the tension of the hectic day.

I woke up the next morning to thunderclaps and wind, drove out to the lake with rain beating at the car. Great. Andy and I wore ponchos and huddled behind the windshield on our trip across the lake. With Paul's help, we hauled the boat out and installed it on the rented trailer during the rainstorm.

Thursday now.

Noon.

August 6.

Two days to go.

The engine missed on the trip across White Bear. The driving rain spotted the new varnish. We used the public launching ramp at the VFW Hall next to Johnson's on the west shore. Then I drove Paul back to Mahtomedi before

Andy and I headed back to St. Paul for the final preparations.

I was exhausted on the drive back to town. Things were not going smoothly. We were cutting the time left too close to the bone.

Back at home, with less than forty-eight hours to go, I installed the interior seating, screwed down the loose floorboards, and then installed a black-ribbed rubber matting over them.

Jennifer had known where to get the matting: from a wholesaler her father's sewing machine company had done business with. In 1938 most Chris Crafts were floored with linoleum so substantial it was called battleship linoleum, of a robin's egg blue swirl pattern. I've seen glimpses of that linoleum, incidentally, in schools, in the back rooms of certain hardware stores, and on the basement steps of homes built in the late 1940s. I've been at cocktail parties in which I pause, trancelike, studying the linoleum on somebody's basement steps, examining a curious clue or connection on my trip through life. Not conducting a search for that exact linoleum was virtually my only concession to convenience; there just wasn't time for that.

At approximately 4 P.M. Friday, August 7, less than twenty-four hours before the show, I ran short of the rubber matting. I could get more by getting to the dealer before 4:30. I set off, tired, sweaty, angry, anxious, and alone. Five blocks from home, at the intersection of Cretin and St. Clair, while waiting at a stoplight, my chest tightened and I felt light-headed. The tops of the trees seemed to dissolve into a lighter shade of green against the blue sky. I swore the street moved up and down beneath the car. I ran through every popular symptom and managed to convince myself that I was suffering a major heart attack.

"I knew it," I said aloud in the car. "Oh, I knew it."

The thought that next occurred to me was this: I don't want to die in the intersection of Cretin and St. Clair in my car.

On the green light I swung left and doubled back home, bent over the steering wheel, my palms sweaty. I either had or imagined to have unusual pains up and down my arms. Only a few more blocks to go. I pulled up in front of the house and went as quickly as possible indoors.

"Jennifer, Jennifer!"

She looked around the corner of the kitchen, not a trace of concern on her face, the phone surgically implanted between her shoulder and her left ear.

"What?" She took her mouth away from whomever it was she was talking to. "What's the matter?"

"I'm having a heart attack. It came on at Cretin and St. Clair."

I got down flat on the living room floor and tried to be calm. I breathed deeply. It felt good. Jennifer stayed in the kitchen, talking on the phone.

"It's 4:10," she sang out after hanging up the telephone. "You have twenty minutes to get the flooring material. You've come this far. Don't give up now."

"Didn't you hear me?" I said, pushing myself up on my elbows. "I'm telling you I'm cashing it in here. I'm having a heart attack, the big one, the big boomer."

"Take Stephanie with you," Jennifer said.

I was off the floor now, telling her to read my lips as I paced around outside the kitchen. "Are you crazy? Take the baby when I'm having a heart attack?"

"Do you think for one minute that I would entrust the baby with you, in a car, if I thought you were having a heart attack?"

Michael De Bakey himself could have arrived on our

doorstep at that moment, examined me, and not offered any more-conclusive evidence that I wasn't having a heart attack. I was having a full-blown anxiety attack. Or had. It vanished quite suddenly, magically—every symptom.

Jennifer and I worked long into that final night, the big garage door open, the garage lights making a spill of yellow light on the dark alley. All of us were out there. The air was warm. I was in the boat, trimming the flooring. It was hard to believe that such rough, major work could have come down to such final moments of trimming, with razor blades and rulers and scissors, the small implements of delicate work. Jennifer was arranging a display of pictures, sorting them on the workbench. Andy and Emily were cleaning the garage, sweeping up long, licorice like strips of trimmed rubber from earlier in the day when I had sized the rubber to the floorboards that I hadn't yet screwed into place. The baby was in her stroller until her bedtime, and then Jennifer pushed her inside. Soon, Andy and Emily also went inside.

Then I was alone in the boat, and the thought overwhelmed me that I was going to make it. It made me grin. I just knew it, and I slumped down inside the boat and leaned my back against the brightly varnished interior siding. I thought of the past two years and was proud of having accomplished it all, thankful for Ray, for Jennifer, for Bud.

I thought back over the two years, average years in the life of an average family, except that I had introduced into our lives the resurrection of a fifty-year-old boat that had come to mean something to each of us. To Jennifer, it meant my presence, my transformation from wandering sportswriter to home boy. To my children, especially Andy, who I am sure would never end up writing about such a thing, it served the useful purpose of introducing them to the notion of my own capabilities with tools and hand-work and labor.

To me, the boat was a connection, probably the last one I would make between myself and Bud. I didn't even necessarily come to believe that I had restored the boat for him. I just did it; I started on it and couldn't, wouldn't stop. It happened to reflect what was most common between us, boats, water, the bottom line of a life disappearing.

Before going in, I turned on the bow light. It glowed red and green in the dark, reminding me of that beer sign glowing in the darkness behind the bar at Vince Guarnera's saloon.

19

I GOT UP AT DAWN ON SATURDAY and then went in and shook Andy awake. Jennifer followed me downstairs. I made what Red Smith once called barefoot coffee, padding around in bare feet to keep from waking the two girls, Emily and Stephanie. I sipped coffee while I glanced at the paper but my mind was on the show. I wanted to be going. Jennifer and I synchronized our plans, and then she hugged me and said good luck.

Andy and I waited out in the alley for Herb Lethert. Herb said he'd follow us out in his big olive-green Chevrolet station wagon. Herb, a mortgage banker, was a buddy of mine since college. He intended to sound the alarm by means of honking and frantic gesturing if for some reason we lost the rig along Highway 7 and managed not to know it. Neither development seemed likely, but Herb had been on hand for some of the less glamorous jobs, including the turning-over process when he performed the role of foreman. I couldn't think of any better distinction than to have him witness the actual launching for the show. I hoped that he, too, thought it was an honor to arise at 6 A.M. on a summer Saturday.

Herb was right on the button, sleepy-looking, one of those guys with a five o'clock shadow no matter the time of day. He drove with one hand, his free hand around a mug of coffee. He helped me hook the trailer to Jennifer's Pontiac and then I led the way down the alley, the eastern sky lighting up over the tops of the houses and the yonder trees and steeples of Highland Park.

We put in at Dick Cole's place on Minnetonka, the trip there thankfully uneventful over thirty miles or so of quiet Saturday morning freeway around the southern rim of the Twin Cities. The car dealerships and shopping malls were just coming to life, with swabbies out in the parking lots hosing down the used cars. They were the same freeways we had traveled coming home from Menth's that July night two long summers ago when the salvaging task seemed so unlikely. Now our cargo was shiny and bright, strapped to a trailer locked properly enough to the hitch.

Cole's place was a dream, a fantasy come true. Cole had a launching ramp adjacent to his boat-building shed/garage at the end of a channel in Gideon Bay, the steep launching ramp strewn with rocks and gravel for traction. Cole did not live on the property but only maintained the establishment there in a retirement setup that provided him with a place not only to work on his boats but also to keep them in the water when he was done with one of them. When I first saw Cole's place it reminded me of New England and then, more specifically, the upriver areas of Detroit, near Algonac, protected channel water, the shelter of land, with the open water beyond the channel.

In 1983, Cole's 1956 twenty-foot Chris Craft Continental won Best Classic Utility and the Real Runabouts Award in the eighth Lake Minnetonka Antique and Classic

Boat Rendezvous. Cole became instantly famous that summer, a cult hero, for the remarkable quality of his varnishing and his detail work—he had removed the thousands of discolored brass screws from the interior bottom planking in his bilge, painted the bilge the original mahogany-red color, and then refastened the screws. He had polished each screw, so that the freshly painted bilge appeared to be riveted with brass. Cole also painted half of the delicate white tachometer needle red. Though unnecessary and even unoriginal, it was an exceedingly effective way to set off the re-faced instrument and the polished chrome ring that houses the tach to the varnished dash.

I got to know Cole through his friendship with Bill Reed, the two of them close old salts. They had worked together in abrasives at the 3M Company—Cole in automotive and Reed in the industrial end—and were now retired. They both experimented with abrasives in their boat restorations: abrasives, epoxies, fillers, light-tack tapes, and sandpapers. Reed, for example, kept his own epoxy concoction in a mayonnaise jar in a refrigerator on the porch of his boat house at White Bear; Reed had spooned me out a jarful of the stuff when Ray and I installed the new stem. Cole and Reed were usually together at boat shows, too, Reed the tall and slender one, Cole shorter and a little blockier, with a nice, agile spring built into his step.

Cole welcomed us, introduced himself to Herb and Andy, and walked around my boat, proclaiming it a winner. He was serious.

"Let's do it," he said.

He hitched the trailer to the front bumper of his new Ford blue-and-white pickup truck and then pushed the boat into the water, which was easier than backing it in. It was a Johnson Boat Works way of moving boats around that I hadn't seen in twenty years. The trailer—the road-worthy rented trailer—tipped and rocked as it rolled over the rocks. I walked alongside, holding the bow rope. Cole didn't make a task of it. He knew every inch of the ramp, even the ramp under the pea-green channel water.

The boat slid off easily and floated slowly backwards. I was holding the bow painter loosely, as though holding the reins of a well-mannered horse. I walked along the dock with the boat, nudging the front of the boat away with the toe of my shoe, Andy doing the same to the stern. We were in. We were, at the very least, thirty minutes from the show docks.

When I was Andy's age, maybe a year or two older, I raced in sailing regattas around Minnesota and Wisconsin. On those weekend mornings, with my boat newly launched in strange waters, my stomach tightened and my senses sharpened so that sight and sound and color were heightened. I remember a water patrol boat casting an eerie shadow on the lee side of a public park at Lake Winnebago in Appleton, Wisconsin. The words *water patrol* shimmered on the flat water. And I remember what it was like to sail around the protected point of the park onto a body of water I could not see across and how comforting it was back then when my father seemed to miraculously appear from out of the horizon in a rented twelve-foot aluminum fishing boat with a ridiculously underpowered outboard motor on the back.

"Storm coming," he said one time when he nosed up to us on Winnebago. It was hot, the air thick. The big lake was uncommonly still and flat; in the distance, to the east, there was darkness. All you could hear was the chatter of the young sailors and the halyards softly brushing and scraping against rigging as the boats rocked whenever a motorboat went by and disturbed the water. Then the water patrol boat went through the crowd of sailboats, a voice on the patrol boat speaking through a bullhorn, ordering the sailors to clear the lake, to get back to shore.

"Tie on," Bud said, "and we'll grab the others," meaning the other X-boats from White Bear. Then he towed about five of us back in and around the point, not much time to spare before the dark line in the distance came moving powerfully across the lake like a dark wall, bringing gusts of wind and hard, driving rain, all of us huddled in our boats on the protected side of the park.

Minnetonka had the same unnerving effect during the regattas there. Minnetonka and Winnebago were sea-like bodies of water compared with the safe and reasonable perimeters of the home shores at White Bear.

Now I felt the same way again, the old stirrings, the utility floating on strange waters that meant mystery and adventure and sometimes even frightening passage. I was chilled from being nervous. Cole admired the boat, giving me easy directions out of the channel, around Solberg Point and then into the show docks in Excelsior Bay. Andy coiled ropes and squared the cushions. He dampened a sponge, too, and wiped the channel slime off the hull sides down near the waterline that was getting flecked with diced green weeds in the channel slop. To save battery power, I squirted a shot of ether into the carburetor, and the engine fired off on the first press of the button. Andy bent over the stern, anticipating exhaust water.

"We got it," he said.

Cole smiled, understanding that it was a scene, maybe a once in a lifetime thing, this moment of the years coming together. Herb, who was hearing the engine for the first time, did the same. I asked them if they wanted a ride, but they said they'd drive over. Cole had signed up to work the docks and tie up the arriving boats. He said he'd see us there. Herb wanted to have his car at the show. He anticipated having to leave before noon to watch his wife play in a tennis tournament. He followed Cole.

Andy and I were on our own. It was a Saturday morning and time was making a loop through the ages.

We backed away from the dock and then got the nose out in a series of tight turning maneuvers—forward, reverse, forward, reverse—in the narrow channel. The channel was weedy, with old cottages converted to year-round places built right up to the edge of the water where there were pilings, moss growing on the pilings.

The wind freshened when we entered Gideon Bay, hard blue water starting to roll between the shoreline and Frog Island. Andy, dressed in sweatpants, a red nylon jacket, and his Detroit Tiger baseball cap, unfurled the stern flag, checking again for the spitting water out of the exhaust. The engine sounded good, but when I nudged the throttle the engine hesitated. Andy and I looked at each other. The engine gave the impression that it would die if it was pushed. It chugged along steadily at idle, but idle, at 1,000 rpms, threatened to be not enough power to navigate the open lake. The rolling swells started to slap the sides of the hull. We pretended to enjoy it, and I instinctively gave Andy encouragement that we would make it, but we were out on big water in a fifty-year-old boat with a troubled motor. I listened to the engine with a cocked ear, as though listening for a sound in the house at night. Two days previously, when we had taken it from Mahtomedi to the White Bear shore, we had had some balking problems, but nothing like this.

So long as the wind came at our side, a chilly wind out of the north, the boat moved along with only a minimum of struggle. We crept along the Excelsior shore and then cleared Solberg Point. Two fishermen, casting from the high swivel chairs in their bass boat, were anchored near the point buoys. Downwind was aces. The boat rolled along in the trailing sea. The show docks were dead ahead. The dew on the lawns behind the docks sparkled in the early sun. We were far enough out that the men on the docks were pipe cleaner figures, small, scurrying here and there to catch the arriving show boats.

An Iowan, Tom Barkema, was coming in alongside me in his 1958 seventeen-foot Chris Craft Sportsman. He was 100 yards off my port side. A classic, clipper-nosed twenty-three-foot Continental, Dave Doner's boat, was behind me. We had seen Doner at a gas station on Highway 7 filling the big tank on his Continental, while we were pulled in there filling the utility's tank. Behind Doner's boat was Steve Merjanian's *Rumrunner*, a twenty-five-foot 1949 Chris Craft Sportsman. The bow of the big Sportsman plowed water that fell off to the side in cascading green fountains.

Cole and Herb were waiting at my numbered slip. My number and a map of the dock had arrived in the mail with the confirmation of my registration. Already, they were playing big band swing music through the speakers up on the lawn between the docks. The volunteers in the striped awning tents on the lawn were doing brisk trade in programs and boat club information. There was a woman dressed in a spangled skirt and a headband with a rhinestone in it. Plastic pennants snapped on lines strung in the yard. The earliest arrivers were browsing and drinking coffee from styrofoam cups.

I turned into my slip and held the wheel for balance as we rolled, back sidelong to the waves now. Andy threw the bow ropes to the people waiting on the dock, the dock high above us because it was a big dock, meant for bigger boats, and then Andy scampered to the stern to throw out the ropes looped through the stern lifting ring.

"Beautiful," I heard somebody say.

And then the voices became a murmuring to me, a blending of pleasant sounds.

"It's a long story," I heard myself saying.

20 〜〜〜〜〜〜〜〜〜〜〜〜

I PUT IN FOR THE FINAL TIME of the year on Sunday morning
of Labor Day weekend, at the same Manitou Island ramp
where she had been launched for the first time in twenty
years about a month earlier. This day was different, though,
cooler, a hint of autumn in the hard blue sky. And there
was no urgency, no audience, no Harry and Randy, no fishermen on the wood-slatted island bridge. It was just Andy
and me, with a piece of business to take care of, a loose
end.

The home waters looked familiar and welcome. The
boat slid easily off the trailer. I was getting to be an old
hand at trailering, not even minding that I had returned the
rented apparatus and was back to the contraption I had acquired with the boat. Andy held the boat to the ramp dock
while I parked the car and trailer in the shade in a gravel
lot on the other side of the island road.

The engine started instantly and then burbled. The
wind was strong out of the southeast. Modest chop—there
were whitecaps out in the main lake—curled around the

island's protective green shoreline and rocked the boat enough at the dock that the burbling grew high-pitched when the stern humped clear out of the water. We shoved away and began our rituals, me standing at the thick black wheel, Andy neatening up ropes and life jackets and setting free the stern flag twisted around its pole.

We chugged along the north-facing island shoreline, the houses dark and cool and Sunday-morning quiet. Damp, velvety lawns spread to the water's edge. We caught a whiff of coffee and bacon on the sweet morning wind. From another age we must have looked, a boxy little boat, sun glinting off its bright work and deeply varnished mahogany, the engine making a symphony of internal combustion. What an extraordinary feeling it was to create the elements of one of my own earliest memories—the passing by of a motorboat on a Sunday morning.

"Take over, boy," I said to Andy.

He knelt on the seat to boost his height and improve his vision. I cautioned him to angle through the waves to minimize the spray. We soon enough left the protection of the island. The waves were bigger. Off in the distance sailboats plowed rough water in the White Bear Yacht Club's Labor Day races. I sat on the engine cover. The wind and sun felt good on my face. At my feet, on the floor behind the front seat, were two trophies, the smaller one a plaque that had black engraved letters on a gold plate bolted to a wood base—"Best Antique Utility Under 20 feet, 1986." The larger of the two was a genuine trophy, a gold speedboat atop a gold pedestal, the "Real Runabouts Award," presented at the Antique and Classic Boat Rendezvous to the boat that best exemplifies its owner's workmanship. Informally, it is known at the trophy that goes to the owner who did his own work; I knew it as the trophy that went to the owner who did his own work with the help of Ray.

We were champions now, going proudly through the same water that had beaded up on this bow light and this windshield thirty and forty years before.

The show seemed ages ago, something imagined or dreamed. It came and went too fast. After it was over I felt just the way I felt after road trips to big events, like a Super Bowl or a World Series. I felt the tension leave my bones after the show. I sensed the nervousness leak out of my system until I was solid again and adjusted and sleeping like a baby, the boat out in the garage under cover and out of the sunlight, its improbable tasks, save one, finally accomplished.

From almost the instant we tied up on the Saturday morning, a crowd gathered around and never thinned out the entire weekend. In many ways it was exactly as I had anticipated during all those hours of sanding and staining and varnishing in the garage back home. The sounds and images and the little tape loops of conversation were as I had imagined. . . .

"It's just like my father's boat . . . in fact all the hardware came from my father's boat. . . ."

"No! You found your father's boat?"

"Now, wait, this isn't his hull, mind you. This is a different hull. I found this hull (I got it from Menth; you know Jon Menth?), and then we found my father's boat. Actually, Menth found my father's boat, too."

"Leave it to Menth."

"Anyway, my dad gave his boat away at the end of the summer of 1962 to settle a ninety-dollar gas and storage bill."

"Oh, no! C'mon!"

"I'm not kidding! It sat for years in a farm field near Princeton. Did you see the pictures?"

Jennifer had rigged a photographic display on poster board, covered with glass. She framed it and then sized her old oil painting easel to the poster board. I set it up on the dock at the show, in the manner of a vendor advertising his wares at a sidewalk arts and crafts show. The pictures ran clockwise around a brief biography of the boat, the first picture showing the complete boat in the driveway at Menth's, two summers previously, the second picture showing the stripped hull as it looked in front of our house in St. Paul after we had had the boat home for a couple of days. The third picture was a tight shot of the bilge under the front seat, showing the leaves and the grease- and oil-encrusted cables and lines.

There was a shot of the old and new stem, side by side against a garage wall, two shots of the spread-open bow of the boat before stem implantation, two shots taken from the stern showing the dismantled transom, a shot of the dismantled front deck showing the rotten king plank, a shot of the boat overturned, a shot of the dash before its repair, and finally, two shots of the completed boat, port and starboard views, one of them showing Paul in his uniform. He was working that summer as a security guard at a teenage nightclub. Paul standing there next to the boat in his dress blues made it appear as though the boat were a museum piece.

Over the weekend I couldn't resist the temptation to stand in the thicket of admirers around the display and listen to their comments, most of them in an astonished tone, the picture of the overturned hull drawing the most curiosity.

"How did he do that?"

I was standing at the back of a crowd on the Sunday morning of the show when a woman reached out to point out something to her companion and knocked the display off the easel. The onlookers gasped. I tried to get through the crowd but I couldn't. The woman reached for the falling poster but it bounced on the dock and then dropped into the water. It somehow slid under the dock as we all shifted to watch it come out the other side, where it was helicoptering downward, like a descending maple seed. It soon enough sank out of sight, too deep for me to go after. It was gone.

The woman who had caused the turmoil apologized, but I assured her that I had duplicates of the photographs.

"Oh, thank goodness," she said. "You've got something very special here."

Jennifer, Emily, and Stephanie came to the show both days. Friends came to the show. Neighbors came, all with their cameras. If I wandered away from the boat on some errand or to get a beer, Andy always stayed behind to run the pump if need be and answer questions. The boat was leaking—not drastically, but enough to be monitored. The pump switch that once was located garishly on the dash had been moved to the facing piece of the front seat, as discreetly within reach as the seat adjustment lever on an automobile. The hole left in the dash was covered with a piece of mahogany cut to look as inconspicuous as possible and resemble a glove compartment door.

My photo display was appreciated but it didn't approach the remarkable stage production of none other than Menth. Not only did Menth have his beautiful 1939 utility entered in the show, but lashed to it and taking on considerable water was an unrestored duplicate 1939 utility that he had just found that summer in western Minnesota. Menth had the two boats entered as a "before and after" display, the first such educational display in the show's history. It was an unbelievably nifty bit of Menth showmanship, a statement, a way to say to the arriving crowds that he was the king. He was rewarded for it too, with a Best Display trophy.

Bud saved his only visit for Sunday afternoon. I could see him through the tangle of legs and arms on the dock. I saw him at the base of the dock near shore, slowly navigating his way down the ramp that led to the dock. His arm was bandaged and still in a sling. He limped. He carried his three-legged stool in his good hand. His friends downtown had taken to calling it his portable bar stool.

He maneuvered through the crowd on the dock. I lost sight of him here and there in the crowd. I froze for a moment. I wanted him to be young again, and maybe the boat was my clumsy attempt to help him to feel his own youth or to inspire in him comforting thoughts to ease the physical pain and disappointment of deterioration.

"Hey," he said, setting his stool on the dock alongside the boat.

"Hey, yourself."

He sat tall on his stool, always proud of his ramrod posture. I wanted to get him into the boat, but the dock was too high. It didn't seem like it, but it had been six years since we first came upon Menth's boat in precisely the same location, the same slip. I had noticed, no matter how much he might deny it, that there was just a flickering of desire in Bud's eyes when he had looked in appreciation at that boat. He was able to get in Menth's boat that day. It was what had started it all really, that ride around the show docks, Bud and Andy and Paul sitting in the back seat of Menth's boat, grinning like clowns for my camera.

Now Bud was confined to his stool; not enough rubber was left in his bones to make the climb down and sit in the boat.

With Bud's arrival and the show's winding down to the awards ceremony, the mood was festive, more relaxed, with friends and neighbors taking turns positioning each other in the back seat for family portraits. Many of them, including my two brothers, stayed around for the trophy presentation late in the day. I had to climb the steps to a crow's nest overlooking the docks and the restaurant tables to accept the awards, and each time I descended I held the hardware aloft, not very bashful about it. Johnny and Paul and Andy took the plaque and the trophy and posed for more photographs in the boat. Then we left the show docks, all of us hunkered down below the dash, avoiding spray and getting pleasant whiffs of the bilge perfume. I gave one last look at the scene on shore, the boats, the pennants, and the people. Good-bye summer.

I kept directing Andy by voice and hand as he worked around behind the racing sailboats. We motored up the east shore of the lake, between the shore and the tack line of the race. It was Sunday morning cool and quiet on our yard, too. We honked in front of the dock and waited for commotion. Paul was first down, then my mother, and then my father, walking with difficulty, but walking.

"Let's put him in the boat, Paul," I told my brother. I didn't intend to make it sound like a conspiracy, but that's the way it must have sounded.

"He won't go for it," Paul said.

"Well, we'll just do it," I said.

"That's right," my mother said. "Just do it."

The boat rocked gently at the dock. Paul held it off with his bare feet. Bud knew we were coming out, but he didn't know what for. I mean, he didn't know that I specifically wanted him in the boat; I didn't know myself until right then.

"Let's go out," I said to him when he reached the

end of the dock. I didn't even want to give him a chance to sit down.

"I don't think so," he said.

"Come on."

"No, I . . ."

"Come on, Papa," Andy said.

"Paul and I will help you," I said.

Paul stood up. Andy held the boat to the dock with both hands, bending at the waist and straining to hold the hull close. My father allowed himself to be helped. Paul used his strength to support him while he stood on the covering board and then I helped lower him. He stood heavily on the blue cushions in the front seat and there was creaking or cracking of wood somewhere. From this standing position he had to collapse himself, so that he was sitting, lo and behold, behind the wheel.

"Drive," I said.

Paul and I sat on the engine box. Andy sat in the front seat. My father made familiar, automatic movements. He knew the oversteering. He knew instinctively how hard to shove the shift lever into forward. Then he gave it gas the way I remember him giving gas to his own utility years before, tapping the throttle lever, all the while watching the gauge until he could tell by the needle on it and by the sound of the engine that he had the throttle where he wanted it. The touch. The respect for boat and water.

He made a picture of movement, a familiar and younger and comforting portrait.

He laughed when the spray got us. I climbed into the front seat, chasing Andy to the back. I raised the windshield but still the spray got us, the spray flew over the glass and made a sparkling mist full of sunburst. Bud headed out toward the windward mark of the sailing race. He made low exclamations of appreciation to himself, murmurings of wonder and of our love, his hands working the wheel of the boat that binds us.

"Andy," he said. "Get the flag."

Epilogue:
The Next Year ⌇⌇⌇⌇⌇⌇⌇⌇⌇⌇⌇

AFTER A WINTER of virtually no snow and very little spring rain, White Bear suffered unusually low water in the summer of 1987. Old *Miss Emily* wouldn't float free of the trailer the Saturday in June when me and Andy and Bud and one of my brothers-in-law tried to launch her at Manitou Island. I intended to use the boat recreationally that summer, keep it at Bud's, on a good used lift that I kept studying the classifieds for but hadn't found yet. Still, after two years of hard and constant work, I wanted to enjoy the boat, but my rush to get it in the water was undoubtedly my first blunder. I couldn't do anything right that summer.

I figured all I needed was help to push the boat free. There was an expectant feeling at the ramp, with more people around than usual. I felt foolish that the task was turning into public folly, the boat stubbornly refusing to slide off that rickety trailer. Bud sat on shore on his golfer's stool and kept pointing his cane at the stern, a parody of a cranky old man. He wore a faded cotton short-sleeved shirt and yellow shorts. His legs were bony-looking.

"Stern's digging in," he kept saying.

I was tempted to go off in search of Harry and Randy. They often worked Saturdays and might have been at their shop just a mile or so away. I decided instead to ask the six teenagers. We had seen them when we arrived, six strapping teenagers hanging around in the bright noontime heat. I hailed to them and waved them over. They walked over quietly, rolling their shoulders, stretching, and went wordlessly to the task of pushing the boat. They had been watching my struggles.

"Rough night last night, fellas?" I asked them. They were sullen and still hadn't spoken, looking hung over.

"We're waiting for our friend," one of them said.

Finally, I understood, the feeling in the air, the mingling of seemingly extra people at the ramp. The six of them said they were waiting for a sheriff's patrol boat to come back from its initial search for the buddy they had lost overboard the night before. They had been partying, driving their boat too fast in the dark. One of them went over the side. They figured they had been between the island and the peninsula when they lost him.

The father of the missing boy recognized me. He wished to believe that I was at the launching ramp in a news-gathering capacity because of his son, that I was there to get the story, his son's story. The father bent to my ear as I worked at the job of launching my boat. He explained to me that he had taught his boy a respect for the water. How could such a thing have happened to his son, he kept asking me. He was standing alongside my boat, knee-deep in the water, talking into my ear, like a sidewalk preacher. He had walked into the lake with his clothes on, not even removing his shoes and socks. Sometimes he didn't make sense, believing his son had merely played a prank by swimming to shore. I looked at Bud up on shore, and he

〰〰 207

slowly shook his head. I had been around other drownings, had grown up with the summer sirens that meant trouble on the water. I was about fifteen when I helped to drag for and then find the body of a sailor, a doctor who had drowned during a race. When we did find him, days after he had gone under, he was brought to shore next door to our house. His wife, dressed in black and wearing a veil, ran through the sand in her high heels and then threw herself over the top of her husband. He was bloated, his skin darkened.

"They'll find my boy," the father of the missing one kept saying.

"I hope they do," I said. "You never know." I said the words slowly, hoping they didn't sound cold.

"There you are," the father said, alongside my boat, "you never know. You're damn right, you just never know." The man's eyes were tired and red-rimmed. The heat and the long night had gotten to him.

All of us kept pushing. The boat resisted. We pushed harder. Finally the boat moved back and then suddenly, surprisingly, filled with water. The stern sunk into the muddy bottom, in waist-deep water. Bud half rose off his stool and said something. I desperately tried to push the boat back.

"Back on the trailer, men," I said.

But we were too late, the boat too heavy now with the lake pouring into it. Dried-out seams couldn't have allowed that much leakage. The only thing we could do was try and get the boat out of the water. My brother-in-law went to his house and returned with rope, a winch, and six buckets. Andy and I and some of the teenagers bailed. The boat shipped water as fast as we bailed. My brother-in-law tied the rope to the bumper of his van, and then I tied the other end to the front lifting ring. Through a long, slow pulling, pushing, and struggling, we got the boat back on the trailer.

Up on the ramp the water poured out of the bottom. One of the rubber rollers on the trailer had crumbled off its axle bracket; we had been pushing the boat over a U-shaped iron bracket that held the roller. As we pushed, the bracket kept furrowing open the seam between the keel and the first bottom board along the keel. Low water wasn't our problem.

"Sweet Jesus," I said, softly. Maybe I was angry. Or maybe it was a prayer for the kid out in the water.

"Judas Priest," Bud said. He craned his neck under the bow the best he could. He looked disgusted. Andy was silent. My brother-in-law loaded his gear back into his van.

The father of the missing boy watched us drive away. He stood on the hot pavement of the ramp, standing in the puddles made from his dripping clothes.

In a week's time the boat dried out enough for me to assess the damage—the long, ripped-open seam next to the keel. It wasn't as bad as I thought. I masked off the seam, stuck the nose of my caulking gun into the gap, and then filled the seam. I let the boat sit for a month in Bud's garage, pretending that I needed to let the caulk cure. I wasn't motivated. I was getting tired from the problems the boat was causing me, the imperfections, the never getting anything accomplished without a hassle. The bum trailer. I cursed myself plenty for not getting a proper trailer to begin with. Unbelievably, we had had the boat three-pointed that month in dry dock, and rather than take that opportunity to get a new trailer, I only replaced the broken roller on the old one.

Paul and I were in the garage out at the lake one night in July—Bud was out in his pontoon boat—when, in a fit of anger, Paul started bitching loud and long, not believing that I could have taken so much care to restore the boat and never done anything about the trailer. He sounded like Randy Zemke bitching about Pete Dunn.

"You're a jerk," Paul said, "you're half-assed."

Paul started banging around in the garage, shoving a lawnmower against a wall, kicking aside rakes and brooms. He hooked the trailer to Bud's Simplicity yard tractor. Off he went through the yard, pulling my boat through the shade, pulling the rig right down to the beach, to launch it right on our very shore. Paul made a sweeping circle in the front yard and then slowly, carefully backed the trailer over the crest of the front lawn and into the water.

"There, you dumb shit," Paul said. The trailer was in just far enough for the bottom of the boat to soak, almost precisely from the waterline down. We could let the boat soak up properly for a couple of days, pump it out, and then easily float it off the trailer.

Taking charge improved Paul's mood. Being home from college for his last summer had been getting to him, reminding him, after a school year's absence, of Bud's sharply declining health, his going in and out of heart failure, his worsening arthritis. Bud was shrinking on us.

"You know how many pills he takes?" Paul asked me before he drove the tractor back to the garage. "The effing pills are lined up, one after the other, all shapes, all colors."

I didn't wait for Bud to come in off the lake to see his reaction to the utility sitting on shore. I covered the boat with a canvas and went home.

There was a storm that night. The storm woke me up, in town. We had moved to a different house that spring.

Our new backyard was bordered by tall pines and blue spruce. The wind in the trees is what woke me. And then lightning flashed and played on our bedroom walls.

I sat up in bed and listened to the storm. Jennifer stirred.

"I wonder if I should call the lake," I said. I looked at the red dial of the clock on the nightstand. It was 3 A.M. What could I have told Paul, get down to the lake and stand guard?

The next morning I called Bud, and he said the boat looked fine to him. I was relieved and told him I would be out later that afternoon.

I didn't find the storm damage until I had peeled back the canvas.

"Judas Priest!"

Waves kicked up in the storm moved the boat back and forth on the trailer all night long. Under the canvas, so that it was not visible to Bud as he looked down at the lake over his morning coffee, was a hole worn into the port side, just back from the bow. As neatly as it it had been done with a saw, a piece of L-shaped iron that supported a winch on the front of the trailer had cut through two side planks. There was a fresh gouge, too, from deck to waterline.

I didn't feel all that angry. I just felt defeated.

I appeared as scheduled at the Bob Speltz Real Runabouts Show in Albert Lea in mid-July, but without my damaged boat. Per custom, I was the show's guest of honor, the defending Speltz trophy winner from the previous summer's Minnetonka show. Speltz graciously insisted that I appear even without my boat. It was a good day, a time of reunion. Tom Barkema, my slip mate from the Minnetonka show, was up from Iowa with his boat. I saw old, familiar faces, Cole, Reed, Menth, all of whom comically suffered with me as I told them the story of the storm damage, the boat riding all night long against a rusty iron bracket.

Tom Juul was there, too. He was showing a special runabout, the same model boat I had in Bud's garage waiting to be restored.

"Recognize that stern pole?" Juul said, meaning the stern pole on his special.

A new pennant was flying from Juul's stern. His stern pole was the antique type, the rich, green-tinted glass globe from the 1930s. Such a pole was incorrect on a special.

"From my dad's?" I said.

"The very one we found under the gas tank," Juul said.

"Think we can ever make a trade?" I asked. At home, I had the less-ornamental correct and original stern pole and light for my special.

Juul said we could work something out. I sat with him for hours, talking about my utility and what I might do. I told him about Ray and how I was too embarrassed to go back to him.

Juul said he'd swing by my house the next day on his way home to Alexandria. He said he'd give me an estimate for the repair. I took hold of his offer as a new beginning. I told him I wanted the engine tuned. I told him a few of the Pete Dunn stories. Twice the previous fall Dunn had stood in the dark outside our family room windows, looking in, startling us. I had had to wave him around to the front door. He stood just out of range of the porch light, as sad-faced as a wounded old hound. I showed him the sheaf of repair bills that I had accumulated after he delivered the engine to me. By the first snow, Dunn quit showing up.

*　　*　　*

I took the boat to Juul's shop on a July Sunday morning that had turned black with storm by the time we reached St. Cloud. A so-called wall cloud moved toward us from the west, then rain. Emily curled up on the floor of the car. The baby and Andy were wide-eyed in the back seat. When the rain hit, visibility dropped to zero. I couldn't even see the uncovered boat in the rearview mirror. We waited out the storm behind a truck stop in Clearwater.

In August, I returned my Speltz traveling trophy to the Minnetonka show. Word travels fast in the boat-crowd underground, and most people at the Minnetonka show gave me a pat on the back when they saw me or stopped to tell me that they had heard about the boat. I found Juul having brunch and sat with him, pouring myself a cup of his coffee. He told me he had only one more coat of varnish to put on my boat and I could come up and get it.

"I'll be bringing a new trailer," I said, for I had had one built in the two weeks or so since I had last seen Juul. "And if you knock twenty-five dollars off my bill, you can keep my old trailer and sell it to somebody for a boat anchor."

Which is what I did at last: I brought the boat home on a new trailer. A repaired boat, a sound boat, a perfectly running boat. I wondered why I had had to make so many mistakes before I got things right. I had one more Labor Day weekend, too, the boat running smoothly for three days at White Bear. I even got Bud in it one more time, for a long, slow cruise around the lake, just the two of us.

Overnight, it turned cold, and fall moved in. We didn't want to admit the possibility that it could be Bud's last autumn.

*　　*　　*

The house at the lake was sold in the spring, in April, after it finally became evident that Bud could no longer navigate around the place. The emptier the house, the more it shrunk. But our marks were everywhere, a pencil sharpener screwed onto a shelf in the back hall under the liquor cabinet, a bell bolted to one of the pillars in the front, a door knocker shaped like an anchor with a brass braid of rope curled around it. I walked around in the final hour in a stupor of sentiment, like someone fleeing a fire and taking nonsensical things. I took the pencil sharpener and the bell and the door knocker, using a dime for a screwdriver. I carried out the garment bags Bud used on his infrequent travels, a trip to New York once with my mother, his spring fishing trips to Canada. Now, either the garment bags were empty or what clothes they did hold seemed uncharacteristically light, like dust. I felt like an intruder carrying those bags, discovering a lightness I had no business knowing.

On the walls between the basement steps were articles cut out of the White Bear Press listing the dates the ice went out every spring. I gently peeled the tape off the walls and put those clippings in my pocket. The paint was a shade brighter behind the old news clips.

At the very end, I learned the beginning. My mother and I sat out on the deck, the lake a mirror of blue memory on this fine and lush noon hour in May 1988. Bud's heart was growing weaker. He left the house at White Bear for the final time on May 5, 1988, for a last hospital stay while the house was packed up and moved. I helped him downstairs that day. The house was in disarray, boxes in every room. He and my mother had taken an apartment in St. Paul, overlooking the Mississippi River, even that view of brown river water a last inextinguishable link to his being.

"We thought it would never end, didn't we?" my mother said, out on the deck.

"You put up a fight about moving out here, didn't you?" I said.

"Your father would never have forced me to move out here," she said. Her indignation had a way of making me tremble more deeply than Bud's anger ever did. "Actually, it was my idea that we make the move."

"No!"

I remembered them looking for a house in town, once even considering a house on Summit Avenue. Those memories were getting hazy. I had carried with me for more than thirty years the notion that my mother became countrified against her will.

"The butcher at Ralph's was the one who planted the idea in me," she said. "I remember talking to him about our plans to move, and he said we should just knock down the cottage and build right there. I told Dad about it. I was the one."

"I'll be damned," I said. "Dave?" I surprised myself by remembering the name of the butcher at Ralph's, the old Masonic-looking brick grocery store up on Mahtomedi Avenue. That place was there when Bud was a boy.

"Not Dave," my mother said, "the one before Dave. Bert."

I had a quick image of Bert, of Ralph's. There was a barber shop off to the left as you entered, then a hardware store and finally, in a bigger, auditorium-like room in the back, the grocery store. The butcher counter ran the length of the back wall. Back then we were summer people, and I remember it being hot in the store but cool back by the counter, back by Bert, a man in a paper hat who convinced my mother to move year-round to Mahtomedi.

"I was concerned about moving out here, sure," she said, "there wasn't any shopping, no freeways, no schools."

"There were schools," I said. "St. Jude's was here before we were."

"Well, schools, yes, but there was a very real sense of being in the country. I didn't like it at first, but I never put up the fuss that people imagined. And now I don't want to leave."

We stared out at the water. My mother would remember the good times in the house behind us. She broke down only once, when she looked for a final time at her elegant dining room and remembered the laughter there over the years. I took her shoulders then and gently turned her away. That's when we went outside.

I'd miss what was out there in front of us now, the lovely blue mirror of memory.

My youngest sister, Terry, who was visiting from Philadelphia and staying at the apartment on the river, was the one who called me. Our nightstand clock said 3:00, the morning of June 2. All Terry had said to Jennifer was that my mother had called 911 for Bud, and then Jennifer turned to me and said, "It's your dad." Jennifer knew. She was weeping silently as I searched in the dark for my pants. My hands were trembling.

When I got to the apartment, it looked like a disaster scene, a fire truck, a rescue truck, police cars with strobes flashing in the horseshoe drive in front of the colonial entrance to the building. Bud was on the floor of the apartment, just inside the door. He was on his back, unconscious. The paramedics were clustered around him and had a breathing tube in his mouth. They were working, pounding hard on his weary chest. I bent down to be near him, but the paramedics moved me aside. One of them reported getting a faint pulse.

My mother watched the scene from the kitchen, resting her chin in the palm of her hand, as though Bud's stoicism had passed in the night to her. She looked at me and shook her head, and I instantly knew her meaning. No, don't encourage me with hope, the false promise of his faint pulse. Bud is gone.

My mother rode to the hospital in the rescue truck, the siren making its eerie whoop in the night. I followed. We didn't wait long. Emergency room technicians worked for an hour or so, but they couldn't sustain Bud's heartbeat. They were good, kind people. They let us in to see Bud as soon as they could, and that's when I was able to hold him and tell him the things I might have said before if we had ever gotten into the custom of straightforwardness. I could almost hear his voice there in that cool, antiseptic room, hear him politely clearing his throat and telling me it wasn't necessary to smooth back his hair or brush from his lovely cheek one of his own involuntary tears.

Two weeks later we had the boat in a show in Alexandria, a show Tom Juul put together. The boats were docked at the foot of the broad lawn in front of the Arrowwood Resort on Lake Darling. Mine was the oldest boat in the water, but other, older boats were displayed on the lawn, including one of them on my old troublesome trailer, the one I had given to Juul. Everything about the show made me miss Bud, the boats, the sky, the rich, summer blue of the water.

On Sunday morning I got up early and took the boat out, alone. It was a wonderful morning, with the wind just freshening from the south. I idled away from the dock, neatening up the cockpit and unfurling the flags, and then I opened it up, faster and faster until she planed on a line for the distant shoreline, the trees and the houses making that familiar optical illusion of bigness. The water slapped at the bottom boards, crisp, hard spray flying off to the sides. The boat had never run better in its fifty years.

I raced along, feeling suddenly like the luckiest man in the world. Smiling, I tapped the throttle lever back the way I had been taught, bringing the rpms down to a respectful Sunday-morning level. I ran my hands over the instruments and controls, felt the smoothness of the wood, admired the brightness of the sun in the glistening varnish.

It was the touching of our hands, mine and Bud's, down through the years, in boats.